Also by Gretchen Stewart

The Choice
Joy Manifesto

Simplicity

Gretchen Stewart

Simplicity

Cultivate a life of freedom,
focus and joy

Sunshine Press

Copyright © 2017 by Gretchen Stewart
All rights reserved.

No part of this book may be reproduced in any manner without written permission except in the case of brief quotations embodied in critical articles and reviews.

Although the author and publisher have made every effort to ensure that the information in this book was correct at press time, the author and publisher do not assume and hereby disclaim any liability to any party for any loss, damage, or disruption caused by errors or omissions, whether such errors or omissions result from negligence, accident, or any other cause. Forms and agreements are included for your information only.

For information about special discounts for bulk purchases or author interviews, appearances, and speaking engagements please contact: howdy@sunshinepress.co

First Edition
ISBN: 978-0-9989726-2-6
ISBN: 978-0-9989726-1-9 (ebook)

Library of Congress Cataloging-in-Publication Data is available

Published by Sunshine Press
www.sunshinepress.co
Printed in the United States of America

To Ken, Sophia, and Cash.
You three are my heart and soul. "Nickday"

Contents

Introduction 1
01 Mindset 9
02 Growth 19
03 Creation 27
04 Focus 37
05 Fluidity 49
06 Curation 57
07 Peace 67
08 Objects 77
09 Earth 83
10 Intention 91
11 Authenticity 99
12 Freedom 111
Bye, For Now 117
Letters Of Triumph 121
Simplicity Principles 133
Acknowledgments 137
About Gretchen 141

Sim·plic·i·ty

sim'plisədē/

Noun

- the state of being simple, uncomplicated, or uncompounded
- freedom from pretense or guile
- directness of expression

– Merriam-Webster

Simplicity

Calm, peace, life philosophy, mindset, anti-drama, freedom, security, joy, creativity, individuality, authenticity, freedom, sincerity, naturalness, lack of pretentiousness, honesty, directness, candor, ease

– Gretchen Stewart

Simplicity

Introduction

I squinted at the quilted earth below me. Was this real? My voice was inaudible under the industrial drone of the airplane. I was out of control. I liked it. Surrendering my life to "Mike" was the easiest decision I made today.

After the count of three we were plummeting to the earth. The wind pushed my skin into my ears and flapped my lips. I had a fleeting thought that I must not look too cute right now as the photographer air-swam over to me to take evidence. I looked down at the little trees getting bigger. This could go very wrong. The wind howled, my guts were commingling with the neurons of my brain. It was a Dali painting come to life, I was in the vortex of an alternate reality.

I wasn't scared.

It was too surreal and exhilarating to be scary. I had no control and yet it was the most liberating experience of my life. My cheeks were sore from the adrenaline-induced permagrin. My father and I went skydiving every Father's

Day for a few years and it was everything. The sweet memories, the bonding, the excitement coursing through our veins and the lesson in letting go.

Learning to let go has led to the most blissful and rewarding experiences of my life and has had a profound impact on my personal metamorphosis. I noticed a pattern throughout my life...each time I let go of the fear that often held me hostage, wonderful rewards came my way. I fell in love, became a nurse, bought a one-way ticket out of the country, moved to NYC by myself at 24, opened my publishing company, wrote this book...

The art of letting go has immeasurable rewards. Sending the micro-manager alter ego that lives in our cerebral cortex on vacation now and then always equals a good time. I know, the gatekeeper of fun in our gray matter is trying to keep us breathing. But what about living, really living?

Letting go = living authentically and unapologetically

Letting go = vulnerability and is scary

Letting go = freedom

Sending my first few books to the editor was scary. Hitting that send button and sharing my thoughts (gasp) felt like walking into first period earth science with nothing on. Naked and vulnerable but conversely free. Free from the confines of clothes. Free to be yourself.

Ok, maybe you don't want to hand your life to some random Mike guy who had the title "Skydiving Instructor" or send your guts on paper to your editor.

But what if learning to let go actually simplified your life and brought more freedom and joy?

Let go.

Have you ever had a moment where you let go and were grateful you did? Getting on a roller coaster? Taking a wrong turn on a street in an unfamiliar city and discovering the most amazing little book shop? Ending a toxic relationship that held you back?

That nagging, whining, insecure voice in our heads that wants to control every freaking detail of our life is just a scared little child. That kid inside feels powerless. We overcompensate by fixating on every. Little. Thing. Yet, the desire to control life is a pipe dream. If we micromanage our whole life, we'll never experience the little wonderful serendipitous things that can happen. Nor the big things like the full-blown adrenaline rush that comes from jumping out of planes!

Simplicity

Belief. Trust. Positivity. Those three things can take us all far in life. What if we believe it will be all right? We trust ourselves? And focus on the positive vs. the negative?

Let go.

Part of simplifying our lives is the art of letting go. Those jeans we keep in our closet for 10 years will never make us happy. Let them go. The self-limiting beliefs that we aren't good enough. Let them go. The books we said we'll read "someday" 10 years ago but still keep on our bookshelf to look intelligent and well read. Let them go. The stuff that we burden ourselves with, that we are suffocating in. Let them go. The constant, nagging desire to buy more, get more, need more... money, things, house size, cars, status, accolades. Let them go. Nobody cares.

It wasn't that long ago that my walk-in closet was overflowing with designer clothes. Accessories upon accessories. I was driving a brand new Audi Q7 and carrying my latest Valentino purse. I had a huge house in a safe, upper middle-class neighborhood. But I was overwhelmed with discontent. I was consuming more and more but it was never enough. Chasing that elusive "American Dream" instead of creating my dream. I was busting my butt doing something I hated for a living because I was convinced I wouldn't feel successful or secure

Introduction

until I was making over 6 figures with my online business. That just wasn't congruent with me.

When I am on my deathbed, I don't think I will be thinking about a nice pair of shoes I had or my beautiful house. I am going to be thinking about an evening I spent with somebody when I was twenty where I felt that I was just absolutely connected to them.

- Tom Ford

I was burnt out. Stressed. Constantly online answering emails and making connections – aka networking – but not loving it. And all for what?

The feeling of discontent was drowning me. I was burdened by a lifestyle of seeking and never attaining. Never would I reach the point where I felt secure. The more money I had, more things I owned... the more I wanted. It was never enough.

I hit a brick wall because of my health (more on that in another book) and because of pure overwhelm. It was then that I made a conscious effort to slow down, quiet my mind and simplify my life. I found that, as I slowed my pace and chose to live deliberately, the happier I was. I am learning and mastering the art of letting go which brings the sweet taste of freedom.

I choose to live a deliberate life. I got rid of all unnecessary things and decided to live a well-curated life. I surrounded myself with beautiful things that I love, I had more free time, my kids played together longer, my creativity blossomed and I felt at peace. I choose to celebrate the art of living and to appreciate the art of simplicity.

In this book I'll share parts of my journey to a more minimalist, creative, fulfilling life. This is not a "how to" book per se, there is no right and wrong. This is what has brought me a simpler, happier life and I hope it inspires you.

I do not have a degree in psychology. I haven't arrived. I'm not the world's best writer. I'm not enlightened. I'm not the most chic person I know. My home doesn't belong in a magazine. I sometimes still get the twitch and scroll through Facebook mindlessly. I impulse-buy my kids toys. Although I know how to cook, I choose not to. Fortunately, I'm a completely flawed human being, which keeps life interesting.

I wrote this book to share my journey and personal perspective on living an intentional, simple and fulfilled

Introduction

life. I'm still on this quest but, as I often do, I put the cart before the horse and decided to write a book about it before I mastered it. I share personal stories, opinions and philosophies I'm drawn to. It's not a black and white/ all or nothing way of living. Pick and choose what resonates with you and just do the best you can. My intention is to bring you joy through my journey.

01 Mindset

January 2009.

My future husband calls me up and says, "Want to move to Costa Rica and buy a bar?"

Wait, what??

My initial reaction was YES please! Then, I cornered him with questions. How, what, who, when, why? We were living in Astoria and planning a move to South Beach, not to Latin America. After a few minutes I started to have trepidations. My reptilian, instinctive brain caught up to the conversation and pulled the emergency brake. The reptilian part of our brain is primitive and primed for survival.

I heard myself say "Yes, but I don't know anything about the restaurant business." And, "What about real estate?" And other silly, logical questions. After a few minutes, I decided to dismiss my boring musings and just go with it. I let it go. So, we sold everything, put some money in a backpack and bought one-way tickets to San Jose. I didn't speak Spanish. I didn't know how to run a business. I had never been to Costa Rica. This subtle (but huge) mindset shift changed my life for the better.

Not only did it exercise my "let it go" muscle, it brought on rich experiences that I wouldn't have had otherwise.

To pursue simplicity and learn the art of letting go is ultimately the quest for freedom. Breaking the chains of ownership sends us into uncharted territory. Freedom Town.

Freedom Town is a place where each person gets to be whomever they want. The citizens have full control over their creative expression. In Freedom Town, no one judges other people. It does not matter what clothes they wear, the color of their skin or the decisions they make. FT is a diverse, forward-thinking and happy town.

Those not living in FT overcomplicate things and live in fear. They live across the river, in Scary Town. They are paralyzed by fear of being judged. They are unfulfilled because they didn't pursue their passions. They wake up each day and trudge to a job they hate, only to fill their houses with meaningless stuff from Amazon. Then they hire a declutterer to organise their crap. Which only makes them neat hoarders vs. messy hoarders. They want their friends to come over and be impressed. But, they never will be. They are too self-absorbed. ST has no poets, no art, no freedom of speech. Just a mass crowd of shumans (sheep and human hybrid) going through the motions, buying whatever the Master tells them to. The Master hides behind a curtain and booms his deep voice via advertisements. His voice permeates everyone's life, yet he is only a scared little man. He is overcompensating for his fear and aching to fill his void with green paper currency.

In ST no one sleeps. They ask themselves... What is that H word? Health? What does that mean? Sun up to sundown they are chasing the dangling cheese in a Wheel Of Hell. They are spinning round and round, calluses broken open and oozing blood and pus, all churning for the Master. Gotta do what he says. Gotta buy what he tells us. Gotta make him his money. Their blood, sweat and dignity sacrificed for the More that never brings them peace.

The citizens of Scary Town look over at Freedom Town with condemnation. Simpletons, they think. Living in a La La Fairyland, singing kumbaya and knitting... They must not have all their synapses firing. But deep inside the fear creeps up... What if they are right? What if I'm doing this for nothing? Won't I be happy if I just sleep a little less

Simplicity

and make a little more money? Even though the citizens of ST are scared that they have it all wrong, they continue their drudgery. They mask their pain with booze, pharmaceuticals and shopping.

Ok, I know I got a little carried away there in that paragraph and may have pissed someone off. It's an exaggeration with a nugget of truth somewhere inside. As humans we are complex, multilayered beings. We often complicate our life internally and externally. Better to make things simple.

Why adopt a simplicity mindset? Because Simplicity is beauty. Simplicity is the antithesis of stress.

It's calm.

Peaceful.

Authentic.

Effortless.

Straightforward.

Have you asked yourself, "Why is adulthood so complicated and messy?"

It doesn't have to be.

Pulling back the layers will reveal an ugly truth. Peeling the onion will cause tears. But with those tears will come a cleansing. A satisfaction and happiness that it's over and done with. It will reveal the real you.

We'll see that consumerism... well, consumed us. Fear of falling behind, fear of boredom and fear of success drove our decisions. We were ignorant and didn't realize that life doesn't have to be this hard. It will become obvious that we use pacifiers such as shopping and wine to soothe us. The realization that we did not have the courage to be the gloriously flawed human being we are, will hit us hard.

This mindset shift and realization will take courage. Most of us dread stripping away the busyness and distractions. They are our security blankets we use to mask our brilliant radiance.

Daily on social media I see people bragging about how they hustle. They brag about not sleeping like it's a badge of honor. Their cloak of busyness is justification for their stress and discontent. Keeping up with the Joneses, if you will.

I was there.

I was too busy to make phone calls. Too busy to complete a project. Too busy to sleep because I was hustling for my pseudo ego-filled dreams. My so-called "passion" was an exasperating cycle of trying to impress others, to get their validation. Chasing more money, more accolades. But what was the tradeoff for these alleged rewards?

- No sleep
- Burnout
- Health issues
- Disharmony
- Stress
- Overwhelm
- Frustration

I was never going to live up to my unrealistic expectations because I was seeking OUTSIDE. The desire to gain others' approval fueled my daily actions. Filling the void with fancy Valentino purses would never bring me joy. I was consuming. All day and all night. I was taking what was being fed to me and letting the multi-billion dollar advertising market dictate what I wanted out of life.

It wasn't until I slowed down and simplified my life that I realized how far gone I was. Although I considered myself less of a consumer than the masses, I was still stuck in the vicious cycle of NEVER ENOUGH. Cutting out the bull opened my eyes. I peeled away the opinions of others. I looked inside myself and found my joy was there all along. My own joy. I stopped caring what people thought and transformed myself into a strong, confident woman. The one I envisioned myself being when I was young... I finally became her.

The change didn't happen until I decided to live with intention. Everything in my life is now on purpose. By focusing and curating what is important, I eliminated the "stuff." The preconceived notions and societal expectations. I cleared off my bookshelves that were overflowing with status symbols. Yeah, I'm well read. So what? Why was I displaying it? I realized that there are millions of people in the world more well read and at the end of the day... nobody cares.

You will become way less concerned with what other people think of you when you realize how seldom they do.

– David Foster Wallace, "Infinite Jest"

The mindset shift continued. Every area of my life was positively affected.

Simplicity

Other people's actions and opinions of me affected my energy and my day. That has been one of the hardest habits to break. I have noticed the old me needed her ego stroked or I'd have one of those "off" days or weeks. God forbid a friend ignored me or I made a marketing move that didn't get enough attention. I'd let it ruin my day, week or even month.

It makes sense though.

It's that reptilian, primitive brain again. That old survival mechanism. Our ancestors kicked people out of the tribe and left people to fend for themselves if they didn't fit in. This would lead to becoming a saber-tooth's amuse-bouche. Instinctively, humans are followers. I've read that only 5% of the population are true leaders. We look for social clues on how to belong and not be ostracized. Many of us prefer to be told what to do, rather than decide it for ourselves. Kind of sobering to think I had so many moments of average. I'm so regular.

The wonderful thing is that we, as a Western society in the 21st century, have it made. We live in an abundant era: food, shelter, clothes are readily available to most of us. With many of our basic needs met, we are free to evolve, grow and rise above flight-or-fight thinking. Now more than ever, we are free to be whomever we want to be. And if we are odd, there is likely a group of like-minded people out there who share our views and tastes. We can shut out the noise of peer pressure and media to live up to our full potential. This is possible!

With my simplicity journey I got to know myself better than ever before. I can see that I was seeking external happiness, which isn't really happiness at all.

When we make major life changes and grow, we expose our flaws. The quieter we become the more we hear. Our awareness awakens to our truth and this can be difficult. I hated to admit to myself that my ego getting bruised could dictate decisions in my life (and moods). I'm going to start E.A. – "Egos Anonymous." I'd bet everyone but Mother Theresa, the Dalai Lama, Gandhi and a few others could use a meeting or two. Most of us need a lifetime's worth. Awareness hurts but it's necessary for long-term growth. Seeing our flaws firsthand strengthens us. It helps us create the best version of ourselves.
If we are honest with ourselves, it hurts so much.

First, we avert our eyes in denial. I'm not like that.

Then, we see red. Our anger fills us. How could I do this to myself?

Simplicity

Then the world blurs through our tears. Why did we hide our true selves for so long?

It's then that the world becomes crisp and clear with the vibrant colors of truth. It's not too late to start over!

Life is no longer a battle. Phew, that was exhausting.

Fierce determination fuels us. We shed other people's opinions and live with joy and authenticity. I am free to be me!

We only desire what we want and need out of life. Living with intention, I ask myself, Why am I doing this? Do I need this? Does this bring me joy?

After culling the old thoughts, expressions, and ideas, we finally hear our voice. The more we stomp out their noise, the louder our voice becomes. Your voice will grow and resonate, strong and unique. That is YOU.

02 Growth

Everything is foggy. I close my eyes and open them again but it doesn't help. My toddler runs up to me and rubs my horizontal legs. I blink the tears out of my eyes and smile through the pain. What a sweet girl, trying to take care of her mommy. Why, why does she have to see me like this? She is so young and full of life and deserves better than a sick mommy.

My legs ache.

I can't move.

I'm so tired.

Oh no, she wants me to read a book. I love that she loves to read but it takes so much energy.

I hate that I dread reading my daughter a book.

I'm so tired.

Oh no, she wants a snack. I have to get up from the couch.

30 minutes until my husband gets home, then he can help. I'm so tired of faking that I feel fine.

Oh no, he brought me flowers!

I love him but now I have to cut them up and arrange them. I don't want to hurt his feelings but I just can't lift my arms right now. The task seems so daunting....

I struggled with ups and downs with my health for about 5 years. I hit a wall after my first miscarriage. It took loads of research and determination and finally finding the right doctor to help me.

The whole time I was ill, I felt there was a reason. Something good would finally come from my suffering, but what? I was open to finding the silver lining but it never seemed to come. Something positive would happen and I would think THIS IS IT!! Then the sledgehammer would knock out my knees and I'd fall to the ground again. I had this nagging feeling somewhere deep inside that I hadn't learned my "lesson" yet. There was some sort of spiritual personal growth lesson I was learning. But damn, I was thick-headed and couldn't figure it out. The whole time I was sick, I was reading personal development

Growth

books with the ferocity of a hungry post-hibernation bear. Constantly consuming and never satisfied. I read about the law of attraction, quantum physics, world religions, and mindset hacks. I was on this quest to "grow." But other people's opinions clouded my personal evolution. I was seeking outward, instead of inward.

Finally, I shut out the noise. It wasn't until I slowed down and cultivated my simplicity mindset that I found peace. I tapped into my inner wisdom by eliminating distractions. I stopped the constant consumption of other people's creations. It was then that I found contentment, happiness and the antithesis of stress. There is wisdom in the world, and there is a time and a place for self-help books and outside influencers. With that said, my true awakening happened when I embraced simplicity. I learned to be true to myself and let go of the judgments and perceptions of others.

At the same time that I was experiencing internal growth, I found some answers and help about my health. My pain and exhaustion slowly dissipated while my mind opened. I was shedding the cocoon and emerged feeling happier and healthier, calmer and more confident, than I had ever felt in my life. Not that I've "arrived" or that I'm done growing. We are always evolving, growing and learning as human beings. Either we are growing, or dying. I'd become the best version of myself thus far and it felt wonderful. So wonderful that I'm writing this book to share it with you. And for you to share with someone you love. And for them to share with someone they love.

It was all so simple, but I had to suffer to see that. My hope is that you don't have to suffer as much as I did to embrace a mindset shift that can set you free. Alas, I do know that we all have to endure pain. Such is life. And those of us who are parents know the kids need to fall down a couple times to learn a particular lesson. I do intend to give you hope if you are already suffering. Or, I can help lessen a blow that may come your way in the future. Simplicity isn't only about culling and curating your life. It's about discovering who you are. It's about finding peace and tapping into your inner wisdom.

Walking through life numb from pacifiers, addictions and distractions is easy. But the avoidance of pain is a mistake. All mistakes lead to our greatest revelations and greatest joys. There is no love without loss. And if you look at the world, the greatest art and discoveries have come from great pain.

The truth will set you free. But not until it is finished with you.

– David Foster Wallace, "Infinite Jest"

Simplifying our life helps us become self-actualized. The unexamined life is not worth living. But it's important to note that if all you do is examine your life to tedium then you are not living either. First, we must strip ourselves to our bare bones and know thyself. Living a life of service is a fulfilling life, but first we must serve ourselves. Then, we must focus outward and ask, How can I serve others? If you study happy people you'll find they spend most of their energy on the people they serve. If you make other people happy, you will feel happier.

Ask yourself, What do YOU love to do? What do you enjoy? What do you teach people about? Who are these people? How do they transition as a result?

After I embraced simplicity and followed my dreams, I instinctively engaged with others. I'm writing books to serve others using my experiences and insight. I also formed a publishing company as another avenue to help lift and empower. Most people want to write a book, but the process can be daunting. I make people happy by helping them realize their dreams. I want you to be triumphant over your pain. I write children's books to give them the mindset tools to tackle the world with an open mind and positive attitude.

There is no right or wrong path. Each of us has moments of clarity and some of us mature faster than others. It may

Simplicity

take 5 or 80 years to peel back the layers and reveal YOU. And that's ok. Because after you do you'll likely change and grow and become a new you. Although we strive for simplicity, we are complex creatures.

But changing our mindset and embracing, even seeking out, growth and change does not have to be complicated. The biggest shift will come from the seemingly subtle habits we can easily ignore. Even in the midst of my illness, I sought out gratitude. Many days it was a stretch. I had to go bare-bones basic and feel gratitude that I was breathing, had a roof over my head, had food to eat. I forced myself to be in the moment and find something to be grateful for. The days I felt better, I was able to look at the big picture and find gratitude for my illness. I trusted that something positive always comes from a negative. And someday, I'd see the good from the pain.

Simplicity is gratitude.

Find something to be thankful for when times are tough. Even when they are good and you are caught up with life, taking a simple moment to appreciate it helps with our personal growth.

There is so much to be happy for when we take moments to stop and notice.

Growth

Children's gut giggles.

The sunlight warming our face.

The first smell of coffee in the morning.

Fresh from the shower sliding into clean sheets.

When you look up and catch the person you love looking at you admiringly.

The stillness at dawn when it's just you and your thoughts.

03 Creation

Simplicity for creators.

I was walking to my locker, heading to 5th period Biology and Mr. McClusky came up to me. "How are you doing today, Gretchen?"

"Uh, I'm ok. You?" I panicked. Why did he want to talk to me? Am I in trouble? At 15 I was insecure, introverted and not prone to chitchat with authority figures like teachers.

"I wanted to encourage you to join Drama Club," he said. "I think you would really like it. We have a meeting after school. Will you join us?"

I'm freaking out. This is my DREAM. All I want to do is be on stage, be someone else but yet finally be free to be ME. How did he know? Why me? What's so special about me? The seconds it took me to answer felt like an eternity while a million excuses came to the tip of my tongue. I stammered "Um, I'd like to. I'll think about it." I'd like to say that I said thank you and had manners, but I may have been too flustered to say those two words.

While we were parting ways he again said, "I think you'd be great, Gretchen. Really try to join."

I didn't.

Flash forward a year. It's time to start thinking about colleges and I research a school a couple hours from home that I'm desperate to go to. It's a school with a great drama department. I dreamt about it daily, what I wanted to do, what it would be like. Time ticked on and my feet grew icy. Everyone asked me what I wanted to major in and my canned response was, "I don't know. Liberal Arts for now?" Bleh. I didn't want them to laugh at my silly dream of being on stage. Weeks passed, months passed, the pressure was on. Would I apply to the school with the great drama department?

Nope. I did not.

I went to nursing school instead and got my R.N. In my mind it was a safe backup. I cared for patients as a nursing assistant during college and found I was very good at it. Nursing was safe, dependable and came easy to me. I told myself a huge lie — that I would pursue acting after college.

Creation

I didn't.

Fear. Much of my life I was riddled with fear and dimmed my own light. I had so many dreams that I held back on because of untrue stories I told myself. "I'm not a creator." "I'm not talented." "I'm not worthy of being on stage." "I can't even freaking sing, who am I kidding?" Self-limiting beliefs ended up crafting much of my adult experience.

We all have those self-limiting beliefs. I'm no different than anyone else. And, we are all creators.

Time went on and I was a talented nurse. I grew in my career and put my dreams on the back burner. I took the easy way out and pursued what I was good at.

A couple of years ago, I shared with my husband the secret dream that had festered in me for twenty-plus years. He supported me 100% and I started taking acting lessons. WOW!! I had NEVER felt so alive. I had found my art! No other form of art I've ever experimented with... painting, drawing, writing... has ever made me feel as if I was so ME. I wasn't scared at all. I was funny and engaging. I was able to let go of inhibitions and be truly me while playing someone else. Acting is a complex form of self-expression that resonates with me.

Simplicity

Before you skip over this chapter thinking you are not artistic or have not labeled yourself a "creator," hear me out. So, you don't want to be on stage. But do you have a creative dream you've buried somewhere inside of you? I bet you do.

You are a creator. We all wore down the tips on our crayons and developed imaginary monsters when we were five years old. As children, all we did was create all day. Sticks were swords. Little brothers were the "boogie men." The stream in the backyard was the Nile. Many of us stuffed our creativity away like we did our dolls when we felt we were "too old" to play with them anymore. Antiquated school systems dulled our unique shine to prepare us for task-based work.

And don't forget Freddy the 4th grader laughing at our story about "The Great Tomato Takeover." We blushed and our voice cracked reading out loud in Ms. Smith's class. God forbid we stand out too much with our ideas. As human beings we want to fit in. But peer pressure and conformity buried our creativity in the basement. It's still there though, under the dusty Atari and backgammon.

As society beat the creativity out of us we told ourselves The Story. You know the one. It says we can't do it. The Story is a lie.

Creation

Creativity takes courage. And unless we have a tremendous amount of encouragement from home or teachers, we succumb to the perils of not pursuing it. This is a tragedy. We are all capable, but many of us simply lack the self-esteem. True growth, innovation and human evolution comes from creators doing their thing, from creating new ideas and new ways to express them. All progress comes from creativity. We get energy from windmills. We have cars that drive themselves. We've been to the moon. We fly in airplanes.

Tapping into our inner creator is everything. Not only is it life-changing for ourselves, but great for society as a whole. Imagine. Being free to be who we are. Inventors, painters, performers, writers and so many more. All creating thought-provoking perspectives honoring our individuality and diversity.

But art, all art, is soul-baring. This intimidates small minds. Sometimes people are scared of creatives and want to hold them back through fear and oppression.

Ok, so we've established that we are all creators at heart and it's for the good of society to be our beautiful, creative selves. So, why is a simplicity mindset imperative for everyone? When we block out the influences of other people's noise we can finally hear ourselves think. When have you had your biggest aha moments? Driving along the highway alone? In the shower? On a walk? Sitting on the toilet? Laying awake at night? The best ideas come from when we are a little bored. The distractions are off and it's just you and your thoughts.

Boredom is a good thing.

Why do we fear boredom when it's beneficial? Well, check out the chapter on Focus. It's worse now, more than ever.

I myself have caught myself doing everything possible to avoid boredom. A long stoplight, and I'd reach for my phone to scroll. Really? I couldn't get through a 2-minute stoplight without feeding my addiction?! The more I ignored the twitch, the more I let myself get bored and ultimately opened my mind up to create. The great ideas just flowed.

The same thing happened for my kids. As I embraced simplicity, I looked around me and saw how many toys and movies they had and felt they could stand to be bored more. So I culled the toys, shut off the movies and let them create their own fun. Rarely do I hear "I'm bored" and if they say it, I give suggestions and they are easily redirected. They create their own games, forts, drawings... the less stuff they had the more creative they became.

Creation

When we look at kids in a typical middle-class household in Western society, what do we see?

We see an overwhelming amount of toys, electronics, cartoons on demand, packaged food, after-school activities, rushing here and there to this activity, that sport, that party and hours of homework.

One of the most important factors in child development is free play. Child-driven play is imperative to strengthen their cognition and emotions, to develop their imagination and to simply learn how to interact with the world.

When I was a kid, the classroom brought me anxiety. I knew the answer but was shy about getting called on and forgetting. I second-guessed myself and wondered, "What if I'm wrong?"

My greatest memories, the ones that molded and stimulated my imagination, came from playing outside. Lost in my own world or the world my friend and I created. Reading my books, drawing and writing.

Unfortunately, a 1997 study from the University of Michigan determined that the amount of spare time available to kids in the U.S. has dropped by 25 percent since 1981, and Boston University psychologist Peter Gray has found that it has been declining ever since. In a 2007 report, the American Academy of Pediatrics found that "much of parent-child time is spent arranging special activities or transporting children between those activities.... Many parents seem to feel as though they are running on a treadmill to keep up yet dare not slow their pace for fear their children will fall behind."

This is very troubling. Kids need to create, make mistakes and figure out how to remedy them. Do you remember a school textbook you read in 6th grade or the time you figured out how to build a dam in the stream in your backyard?

A 2014 study from the University of Colorado found that children between six and seven who engaged in less-structured activities like imaginative role-playing, reading for pleasure, and playing board games and tag demonstrated greater "executive function," or the ability to organize their time, initiate tasks, and achieve goals without external direction. Those of course are the skills which help build self-reliance and success later in life.

Today, it seems that there is a fear of letting kids just BE. We don't want to let kids out of our sight, yet statistics show that crimes against children have decreased. We get messages from the news and authorities that it's negligent to let kids roam free. While no one wants their kids to be unsafe, giving our kids some level of age-appropriate trust instills confidence and self-sufficiency. It allows them to explore their universe and sort things out, like they've done since the beginning of time. Also, "free play" or being a "free range" kid doesn't mean running through town shirtless and shoeless all day and all night. It can simply be having time at home (nature is better though) where kids appear to be unsupervised (within earshot) and the activity they are doing unfolds organically, whether it is reading for pleasure, board games without a parental moderator, or role playing. They are just kids being kids without the bombardment of social activities and media. There is no rule book to raising kids but learning to be self-reliant and fostering creativity can only be beneficial to them.

As a society we are evolving and we will soon no longer be industrial drones doing simple task-oriented jobs. The jobs of the digital age will be creative problem-solving careers. Seth Godin, the best-selling author of "Linchpin," "Tribes" and "Purple Cow," makes this point strongly. "Why do we believe that jobs where we are paid really good money to do work that can be systemized, written in a manual and/or exported are going to come back ever?" he asks. "The internet has squeezed inefficiencies out of many systems, and the ability to move work around, coordinate activity and digitize data all combine to eliminate a wide swath of the jobs the industrial age created…" The more we can foster our future generations' creativity, the better prepared they will be for the future.

You are a creator.

We all are.

Filling our days with distractions hides our potential. A fear-based society holds us back from showing what our minds can do.

But, we need you to be you.

Shut off the electronics. Stop the twitch. Embrace simplicity. Let your mind wander and come up with brilliant ideas. The world needs innovators and thinkers. Our children need you to set an example for them.

04 Focus

I roll over and look at my phone. Sweet. I don't have to get up for 10 more minutes. Laying on my right arm I open my email and skim. Open Instagram and skim. Then Facebook and skim. I read an article, look at pics, scroll through my notifications. I am down a rabbit hole, from studying eyeshadow application methods to quantum physics to natural remedies for increasing energy. Oh shoot, twenty minutes have gone by and now I'm late. I hop out of bed and begin my morning rush feeling depleted before the day has begun.

I was electronically addicted. Electronics stimulate areas in the brain, releasing pleasurable chemicals that are associated with the addictive response. That is what makes it hard for us to shut off electronics.

Before embracing simplicity and learning to focus I also was chasing the flashing lights. My brain was physically addicted while my self-deprecating mind needed to constantly compare. I stopped creating my own reality and consumed others.

While transitioning to a simpler life, I studied what the most influential and intelligent people of the world did. There was no way they were scrolling through Facebook and staring at pretty Instagram pics as soon as they woke up. I knew that in my gut.

I learned a ton from Tim Ferriss, whose podcast was the No. 1 business podcast on all of iTunes in 2016. He's interviewed hundreds of the most powerful people in the world. He specifically asks them how they start their mornings. Well, they are not like 80% of the population that check their smartphones within 15 minutes of waking up. Instead, they seek out their subconscious creativity by meditation and/or journaling.

So now I do, too.

Research confirms that the prefrontal cortex is at its most creative and active immediately following sleep. Your subconscious mind has been working hard while you sleep, making connections and working through feelings and problems. Although our brains are still wired for basic survival we are also able to consciously think and stress about life. We get on social media and focus on the life we don't have and are concerned about our social statuses. But if we are able to control that subconscious instinct, we can rise above.

One person Ferriss interviewed is Josh Waitzkin, a former chess prodigy and tai chi world champion. Waitzkin said that he now uses his morning routine to tap into subconscious breakthroughs and connections he experienced while he was sleeping. Waitzkin meditates and journals afterwards. Instead of consuming, he creates. This is how he gains higher realms of clarity, learning, and creativity—what he calls, "crystallized intelligence."

Why does embracing simplicity help us focus? And why does increasing our focus make us happy?

In society today we are going from one stimulus to another. We are constantly seeking more dopamine-releasing experiences, such as notifications on Facebook, incoming emails and retweets. There is a constant buzzing in our pockets, and we want more.

But we get stupid if we don't focus. Multitasking causes a greater decrease in IQ than smoking pot or losing a night's sleep, found a recent study by the Institute of Psychiatry at the University of London. Other than with music, which doesn't count, we need to stop overloading our system and focus on one thing at a time. Step away, get fresh air, daydream, look out the window and when you focus turn off distractions like email and your phone. What do I do? I simply make a to-do list with two things that need to get done that day and spend my full energy accomplishing that.

Decreasing our media consumption and starting a digital detox can break our addiction and increase our ability to focus again, thus increasing our happiness.

Besides being more time-efficient, focusing and being in the moment is a meditative experience. The more we practice this, the more we get in touch with our inner selves. We are able to shed our ego and get to know ourselves better. Introspection is an intellectual tool that we can all use to elevate our existence. What increases our focus even more is practicing meditation? The scientific benefits of self awareness and mindfulness are extraordinary.

It's safe to say that many of us suffer due to our thoughts. We often spend our lives lost in thought, often worrying or negative self-talk. These detrimental habits keep us blind to the beauty of the human experience. If we want to rise above the suffering, we have to have the intellectual courage to recognize and change our bad habits. Once we learn to concentrate we can see how we wander around in a distracted state the majority of our lives. Unless you are thinking about rainbows and puppy dogs and deep innovative thoughts all day every day, then you are like me. I have this silly inner conversation that if broadcast, would be deeply embarrassing and utterly boring. There is a Buddhist theory that suffering is thinking without knowing you are thinking. To be lost in thought and not know there is an alternative can be hell.

A thought is just a thought. Have you ever been angry about something like getting cut off on the way to work and eventually forgotten about it? Then you go on with your happy day until you remember it again, and then you get fired up again? You DECIDED to be angry, your mind did not remember until you told it to be angry. There have been studies on happiness and there are many people who are in deprived circumstances but are truly happy. The 2017 World Happiness Report noted that, in Western societies, diagnosed mental illness emerges as a more important factor in our happiness than income, employment or physical illness. Our mental state brings more happiness than money. Conversely, how many millionaires and billionaires do you see complaining about trivial matters and a deeply unhappy in life? Our minds define how we react.

Adopting simplicity in our mindset can bring us freedom and bring us closer to experiencing daily joy. Using the tool of mindfulness to shut out distractions, we can have positive effects on emotions, perceptions and cognition. We literally can engineer functional and structural changes in the brain. With mindfulness we can embrace the moment and have passion for the simple things. We experience life clearly and can discern what is real at the moment. Not everything we see or hear is exactly what the person next to us sees or hears. Our individual life experiences influence our thinking.

> For the science nerds like me:
>
> With new technology we are able to finally start proving what the ancients knew long ago – that meditation and mindfulness helps your brain! We still have so much more to learn but here is what we do know: mindfulness and meditation thicken the hippocampus (the learning and memory portion of the brain). It also decreases brain cell volume in the amygdala, which is responsible for fear, anxiety, and stress. In 2011, Sara Lazar and her team at Harvard found that meditation improved mood and well-being.
>
> A study at Johns Hopkins by researcher Madhav Goyal and his team found that the effect of meditation was moderate and comparable to antidepressants. There was evidence of improved anxiety, depression and moderate elimination of pain.

When I discuss meditation, it does not mean you need to sit down and chant. Instead, think of it as brain training to increase awareness, to be mindful. To further simplify would be deeply embarrassing and utterly boring. There is a Buddhist theory that suffering is thinking without knowing you are thinking. To be lost in thought and not know there is an alternative can be hell.

A thought is just a thought. Have you ever been angry about something like getting cut off on the way to work and eventually forgotten about it? Then you go on with your happy day until you remember it again, and then you get fired up again? You DECIDED to be angry, your mind did not remember until you told it to be angry. There have been studies on happiness and there are many people who are in deprived circumstances but are truly happy. The 2017 World Happiness Report noted that, in Western societies, diagnosed mental illness emerges as a more important factor in our happiness than income, employment or physical illness. Our mental state brings more happiness than money. Conversely, how many millionaires and billionaires do you see complaining about trivial matters and a deeply unhappy in life? Our minds define how we react.

Adopting simplicity in our mindset can bring us freedom and bring us closer to experiencing daily joy. Using the tool of mindfulness to shut out distractions, we can have positive effects on emotions, perceptions and cognition. We literally can engineer functional and structural changes in the brain. With mindfulness we can embrace the moment and have passion for the simple things. We experience life clearly and can discern what is real at the moment. Not everything we see or hear is exactly what the person next to us sees or hears. Our individual life experiences influence our thinking.

> For the science nerds like me:
>
> With new technology we are able to finally start proving what the ancients knew long ago – that meditation and mindfulness helps your brain! We still have so much more to learn but here is what we do know: mindfulness and meditation thicken the hippocampus (the learning and memory portion of the brain). It also decreases brain cell volume in the amygdala, which is responsible for fear, anxiety, and stress. In 2011, Sara Lazar and her team at Harvard found that meditation improved mood and well-being.
>
> A study at Johns Hopkins by researcher Madhav Goyal and his team found that the effect of meditation was moderate and comparable to antidepressants. There was evidence of improved anxiety, depression and moderate elimination of pain.

When I discuss meditation, it does not mean you need to sit down and chant. Instead, think of it as brain training to increase awareness, to be mindful. To further simplify this, take note that mindfulness requires no beliefs, traditions, lighting candles or sacrificing sheep. It's merely a tool, a simple practice to increase our concentration and alertness in life. Have you ever lost yourself in your work or something you love and looked up and been shocked that two hours slipped by? You were being mindful in the moment, completely and utterly in focus after you lost your perceived sense of self.

Cutting through your illusion of self is an important part of elevating your existence. Your sense of self can be a painful misperception. The Ego is comparing itself to others and always wanting more of everything in order to feel important. Sometimes, we must stop all the overthinking and just be.

There is an old parable, in a Buddhist text known as the the Sutta Pitaka, about a man who was wounded by a poison arrow. His family brought him to a surgeon but he would not let the surgeon remove the arrow. He said, "I will not let this arrow be taken out until I know who shot me; whether he is a Ksatriya (of warrior caste) or a Vaisya (of the trading or agricultural caste) or a Sudra (of the low caste); what his name and family may be; whether he is tall, short, or of medium stature; whether his complexion is black, brown, or golden; from which village, town or city he comes. I will not let the arrow be taken out until I know the kind of bow with which I was shot; the kind of bowstring used; the type of arrow; what sort of feather was used on the arrow and with what kind of material the point of the arrow was made."

The point of the parable is clear: More thinking is not always the answer, especially when we examine the quality of our thoughts. Fueling the ego can be to our detriment. Instead we can learn to observe our consciousness between deliberate thoughts. We can cut out the automatic and often harmful thoughts and give rise to your self, your YOU. Finding and hearing ourselves will mean we are no longer hostage to our self hating, judgmental or angry thoughts.

Removing the distractions and embracing simplicity helps us have reverence for the ordinary. We are also free to unconditionally love ourselves and others without the cloud of negative societal opinions tainting our views. Neurosis is erased. Made-up illusions are removed.

One day I was driving in upstate New York, singing DMB's "Too Much" at the top of my lungs (don't judge), and I saw a baby elephant on the side of the road eating grass. I was shocked. Did it escape from a zoo? Was it someone's pet? Am I losing my mind? All ran through my head in a matter of 0.5 seconds. Then, I realized it was a simple optical illusion. Darn tree trunk was playing with my mind. My brain was convinced it was seeing a safari animal in Saranac Lake and was trying to logically justify it. How can we see something so clearly in our heads even if it's not logical?

Optical illusions reflect limitations in our perception of physical reality. Remember the viral dress story that circulated on the internet circa 2015? Even the Washington Post published a story, which was headlined: "The inside story of the 'white dress, blue dress' drama that divided a planet." People couldn't agree if the dress was white and gold or blue and black (it was white and gold to me). Ultimately, the debate was about perceptual neuroscience. People were riled up. Actor and writer Mindy Kaling tweeted on February 25, 2015, "I think I'm getting so mad about the dress because it's an assault on what I believe is objective truth."

The problem The Dress brought up is that there is a reality but sometimes our brains don't give us access to it. This uncertainty can be scary or exciting depending on how you look at it. Things do not look the same to everyone. There are billions of cells and connections that are needed just to perceive light, let alone everything else that makes up our human experience. We rely on our perceptions to make decisions, they serve us as we move through life. It's bananas to think we sense light but don't see reality. But that is in fact the truth.

To take this idea a step further: What if your perception of self was wrong? Let's say it was distorted by the divorce of your parents. You react by feeling unwanted, and overcompensate by looking for validation.

Yes, our perceptions in life are based on our individual experiences and subject to change. But once you realize this fact, you can take control! This knowledge helps us understand our behavior and make better decisions.

Sometimes removing the distractions is not enough - we have to remove a preconceived idea of who we are and erase our self-limiting beliefs. Cutting through the garbage that has filled our minds helps us focus and gain incredible clarity in life. Mental creation always precedes physical creation. Before a building is physically constructed, there's a blueprint.

Your thoughts are the blueprint of the life you are building one day at a time. When you learn to channel your thinking—both consciously and subconsciously—you create the conditions that make the achievement of your goals inevitable.

You are the designer of your destiny. This simple routine will help you crystallize where you want to go, and how you will get there.

Behind every decision is an individual, and behind every individual is a perception. A perception based on what we see and what it means to us.

– Tom Cornwall, business consultant

Adopt a "let it go" approach. Decrease outside influencers. Decrease consumption. Understand that your perceptions influence your thoughts and your "perceptions" may be jaded. Stop overthinking.

For big problems, use the Ernest Hemingway Approach. When the novelist wrote something, he would leave a portion for the next day instead of trying to get it all out at once. He'd enjoy his evening and let his subconscious do the work while he slept at night. Stressing and thinking about a problem before sleep is using our conscious brain vs letting our unconscious brain kick in. The stress just raises our cortisol levels and decreases our melatonin production, which inhibits reparative sleep. We need quality sleep every single night for our body and mind to

Simplicity

repair themselves... and for us to be the best, brightest, happiest and healthiest versions of ourselves. In a simple life, sleep is a priority.

05 Fluidity

Be fluid like a river.

I was ready to go home. My book was calling me and I needed to finish it. Groggy from the carb assault on my digestive system, I found the thought of my bed very tempting. But everyone else wanted to "go dancing." And my FOMO – Fear Of Missing Out – was battling my sleepiness. FOMO has a negative connotation for a good reason, but once in awhile there is a benefit to it. I conceded but only grudgingly, and went to hear this new band they were talking about. Once there, I ordered a water and sulked.

But then things changed. The music penetrated my body first. I softened. My feet started tapping. My butt started wiggling. I may have even done the white girl finger-snap but I'd never admit it. Next thing you know, we were all dancing the night away. I was Lost in the music and the moment, dancing and sweating and living. I became fluid like a river. Thus, my existence was elevated.

Simplicity

I can think of a million times that I was rigid and set in my ways to my detriment. And then I can think of another million where I was fluid like a river and it was always positive and often profound. Letting go of plans and preconceived notions and going with the flow can feel counterintuitive at first. You want control. You want knowledge. You want to know what to expect. You want to outthink the world. You want no nasty surprises.

I get it.

The crazy thing is, letting go gives you more control.

What's more important? Controlling what you do on a Friday night or controlling your emotions? When we let go, be fluid, we are ultimately empowered to choose our attitudes. And remember, thoughts become life.

Keep your thoughts positive because your thoughts become your words. Keep your words positive because your words become your behavior. Keep your behavior positive because your behavior becomes your habits. Keep your habits positive because your habits become your values. Keep your values positive because your values become your destiny.

– Mahatma Gandhi

Fluidity

***

My relationship:

My husband and I dated briefly in our 20's and then amicably went our separate ways. Serendipity brought us back together in our 30's and we brought more life experience, past relationships and preset expectations to the table. I had the additional baggage of a heartbreaking divorce which caused me to be guarded. So, what makes us work? Fluidity. Bickering, fighting, hurt feelings, expectations, can haunt any relationship. But when you release the stubbornness (all while honoring your morals, ethics and values) and loosen up a bit, the relationship is easier. Every time either one of us starts to put our foot down about something, we ask ourselves, does it really matter? Do I want this a certain way so much so that it upsets the person I love? Do I care that much? Am I just being difficult? 99% of the time, we realize that we don't care enough to hurt the other one. We pick and choose our battles, which makes for an easy, healthy, happy relationship.

Our marriage is fluid like a river. We bend ourselves around the rocks, flow over and under fallen trees. We are more powerful together. We are strong like a raging river. We are flexible like a river. There is so much we can all learn from studying the river.

When we adopt a simplicity mindset, we are fluid. We do not major in the minor things. We all understand that bad things happen, roadblocks and mistakes are a part of life. The sooner we accept that, the calmer we feel.

Knowing this, we can rise above.

So many of us are stressed and overthink every little move we make. We put certain expectations on a pedestal. We are rigid and close-minded. Decisions are often over-complicated and we are often paralyzed with fear. Since I've accepted the fact that unfortunate events happen and learned that there really is a silver lining in everything, the stress in my life has dissipated. Unless of course you talk to me at 8 a.m. when I'm trying to get my daughter ready for school.

I have found that I worry less and trust more. I trust myself, the Universe, life. I may pout when I hit those roadblocks but after I get over myself I seek the silver lining.

Be a lover, not a fighter. Life does not have to be a battle.

Soon after launching my children's book series, I started seeking an illustrator. I loved the first two I saw; their art and their personalities were congruent with mine. But they were quite a bit out of my price range. I was so dejected. I wondered, how could I bring my vision to life?? I mulled it over, pouted for about an hour, then let it go. The stress was gone as I knew an answer would come to me and a few weeks later it did. A friend, an established artist, said that the messages throughout the books were near and dear to his heart, and he wanted to collaborate on the project. He had had a rough year and was ready to take artistic hold of something and run with it. It was a perfect collaboration with a friend that made the project much more meaningful. He was helping me and I was helping him.

When we are rigid with our ideals and expectations, we will often be let down and stressed. When we adopt fluidity and letting go into our work of art – aka life – the magic happens. We learn lessons, we are open to new experiences and we often find deeper, more meaningful relationships.

Often our thinking gets muddled when we compare our journey with other people's. We see them signing book deals, delivering speeches and getting promotions, and our self-talk becomes nothing but negative bashing. We degrade ourselves because we aren't succeeding as fast as they are. Again, if we use our simplicity mentality to heighten our existence, we will see the truth. We learn that there is not one specific path to success and we can-

Simplicity

not compare ourselves to or replicate others. Those paths would fail. Our true excellence comes from our own story, our own self-expression and following our own path.

The distraction of comparison holds us back from seeing this. Shutting down the negativity enlightens us. This ultimately elevates our thinking, and we rise above the little day-to-day stresses.

*I've reached a point, where I no longer
believe I am unworthy of greatness,
If the people I'm surrounded by, aren't
In Tune with my growth, I'm happy to let go,
If the job I'm working, isn't bringing out the best in me,
I'm happy to find something that will.
If I complain about one thing, I must be grateful for 2 more.
if I can't always have everything I want,
I'll make damn sure I have everything I need.
If life's Thunder hands me tears, I'll be sure to laugh
through it.
If I lose some, I trust it's because i am about to win more.
If there is darkness, the light is almost in reach.
Every obstacle, is the gateway to conscious livingand every
heartache is the gateway to the most empowered love you
could feel.*

– Nikki Rowe, "Once a Girl, Now a Woman"

Fluidity

they were quite a bit out of my price range. I was so dejected. I wondered, how could I bring my vision to life?? I mulled it over, pouted for about an hour, then let it go. The stress was gone as I knew an answer would come to me and a few weeks later it did. A friend, an established artist, said that the messages throughout the books were near and dear to his heart, and he wanted to collaborate on the project. He had had a rough year and was ready to take artistic hold of something and run with it. It was a perfect collaboration with a friend that made the project much more meaningful. He was helping me and I was helping him.

When we are rigid with our ideals and expectations, we will often be let down and stressed. When we adopt fluidity and letting go into our work of art – aka life – the magic happens. We learn lessons, we are open to new experiences and we often find deeper, more meaningful relationships.

Often our thinking gets muddled when we compare our journey with other people's. We see them signing book deals, delivering speeches and getting promotions, and our self-talk becomes nothing but negative bashing. We degrade ourselves because we aren't succeeding as fast as they are. Again, if we use our simplicity mentality to heighten our existence, we will see the truth. We learn that there is not one specific path to success and we can-

Simplicity

not compare ourselves to or replicate others. Those paths would fail. Our true excellence comes from our own story, our own self-expression and following our own path.

The distraction of comparison holds us back from seeing this. Shutting down the negativity enlightens us. This ultimately elevates our thinking, and we rise above the little day-to-day stresses.

*I've reached a point, where I no longer
believe I am unworthy of greatness,
If the people I'm surrounded by, aren't
In Tune with my growth, I'm happy to let go,
If the job I'm working, isn't bringing out the best in me,
I'm happy to find something that will.
If I complain about one thing, I must be grateful for 2 more.
if I can't always have everything I want,
I'll make damn sure I have everything I need.
If life's Thunder hands me tears, I'll be sure to laugh
through it.
If I lose some, I trust it's because i am about to win more.
If there is darkness, the light is almost in reach.
Every obstacle, is the gateway to conscious livingand every
heartache is the gateway to the most empowered love you
could feel.*

– Nikki Rowe, "Once a Girl, Now a Woman"

Fluidity

What is a river?

It's flexible. It flows wherever it desires. It changes direction and speed based on necessity or its wishes. It's strong. Free. Ever changing. Powerful.

Your body is 50-65% water. When we are fluid, we are in our natural state. Be you.

Society promotes rigidity and stress. Becoming one with external forces and demands makes us rigid. We have a hard time handling change when we are guided by stress. We cannot control outside forces but we can control how we react to them. Instead of being fragile, rigid, easy to break–be fluid like a river.

A river cannot be broken. It is strong and the center of life. It knows its power, no one can take it away.

Same for us.

When we become fluid and stop forcing things, we become calm and accepting. We flow with life. We stop giving into the demands that make us sick and we open ourselves up to possibilities and opportunities.

We surrender. Trust. Let go. Be free. Like a river.

06 Curation

I walked into their house. Went past their vacant front "sitting" room. It was sterile and untouched, with tchotchkes everywhere. The couch was covered with doilies and was hard as a rock. It was not meant to sit on, only to look at.

We went to the living room, which had lived-in furniture. There were piles of newspapers, magazines, books, knickknacks and grandkids' toys. After chatting for a bit we sat down to dinner and used their everyday plates while staring at the china cabinet full of dusty special-occasion dinnerware. They had three junk drawers in the kitchen filled with just-in-case things.

We talked. About them retiring. About how they wanted to start traveling. Finally, they'll buy an RV and explore. Then, they complained. About the price of gas. The neighbors. Their friends. Their jobs. Their weekends spent shopping at garage sales and then Costco. How they've filled up their garage and anticipate buying a shed for their "stuff." To accommodate their stuff they park in the driveway and endure suffocating heat in the summer and snow and ice removal all winter.

I couldn't breathe. My head pounded. My eyes ached from doing the inner eye roll over and over again. Were they allergic to my positivity? Why was I wasting my breath? As the droning continued my mind wandered. At what point can I leave without looking rude? Why is it so hard to stay positive in a negative atmosphere?

Their existence was the antithesis of a well-curated life.

An extraordinary life doesn't just happen:
it is constructed, crafted, curated.

- Joshua Fields Millburn & Ryan Nicodemus,
authors of "Essential" and "Everything That Remains"

Living a well-curated life is living the good life. This isn't unattainable or only for the uber-wealthy. We can all make this shift. We can all decide we want to sort through and intentionally choose what we allow in life. Living like the couple above and drowning in clutter and negativity doesn't have to be life. We can decide to surround ourselves with only those things that we love and value.

Curation

This does not mean having only expensive, beautiful, "Made in France" items. It's looking at each item and action in our life and asking if this makes us happy. Are we grateful for this belonging or activity?

I walked into my closet to pick my outfit for the day. It didn't occur to me until after my simplicity journey that the 6' x 6' room was bigger than a worker's family house in Nepal. Instead, I ignorantly looked through everything, exasperated that I had "nothing to wear." Too fancy, too tight, too cheap, the strap is wonky... I had an excuse for everything. I had a ton of clothes that didn't suit me. I ended up picking what I wore once or twice a week and moved on.

This was before I curated my life. Everything in my life... not just my clothing and belongings.

B.C. (Before Curation):
I kept people in my life out of loyalty and kindness, afraid to hurt their feelings. Sometimes just because they liked me and oh boy, do I like to be liked. Some people I hung onto at arm's length, but I still hung on, even if they had a negative vibe, were filled with drama or simply rubbed me the wrong way.

A.C. (After Curation):

Curating the people in my life was hard to do, especially for a people pleaser like me. But I was determined to simplify everything and carefully spend my energy where I wanted. I focused on developing friendships with people that I admired, were smart and kind, and had other qualities I valued (and sometimes I myself needed more of). That old quote, "You are the sum of the five people you spend the most time with," is true. My circle of good friends grew smaller (while still maintaining acquaintances and not burning bridges) yet more rich, meaningful and interesting. Even in my spare time I decreased my mindless social media consumption and spent quality time with podcasts and books.

B.C.:

I held onto ideas like a child holds a balloon about to slip away into the sky where the helium desperately wants to go. These ideas were meant to be let go where they belonged... drifting into the universe a long way away from me as they did me more harm than good. Ideas like these: "You aren't a good writer." "You aren't coordinated enough to play tennis." "You are introverted and uncomfortable." "You are average." "You need to look like a fitness model to be pretty." "Your ideas aren't revolutionary enough to make an impact." "You need to get your Master's and follow societal expectations to fit in." All of these detrimental thought-beliefs needed to be sorted through and discarded. I curated my thinking process.

A.C.:
I let go of that balloon and watched those negative beliefs vanish. Each time they tried to creep back into my mind, I just dismissed them. Yes, this was hard at first but grew easier over time. My energy, the people in my life and my thoughts were controlled.

Amazing changes in my life happened after curation. (Well, let me clarify, I'm still in the process of curation. As I said before, I have not arrived as we are always on a journey of growth.) I now had a calm, drama-free life, and I also realized that my fears had dissipated. I stopped doubting that I was good enough to do this or that. By releasing this negativity and surrounding myself with "can do" people, I:

1. Fearlessly opened a publishing company not knowing how to run it but figuring it out along the way. I spent hours with mentors and researched and subsequently grew the business.
2. Began hosting retreats in exotic locations, teaching workshops and giving people the week of their lives.

3. Agreed to speak at a women's conference in Boston with 11,000 attendees.
4. Started my nonprofit Élan Project.
5. Launched a private Joy Of Living Mastermind to empower other women.
6. Wrote this book, my children's books and "The Choice," a book I co-authored that is eleven stories of ordinary people choosing extraordinary lives.

Conquering the fear of what other people think was for me the ultimate freedom. I also vanquished my fear of creating, growing, evolving. I stopped fearing success and failure, which together had previously left me paralyzed.

Whatever roadblock I hit, I just took it in stride and made big decisions daily. This isn't to pat my back. It's simply because I was now in harmony with myself and I had curated good relationships that lifted me higher.

When we surround ourselves with people who believe in us, read books about incredible people who have overcome obstacles and achieved amazing things. We just assume that we too can do anything. All of us can do anything we want with enough hard work, perseverance and grit. When we let go, life begins to truly happen.

Living a well-curated, simple life helped cure me of the need for immediate gratification. The old me wanted "success" right now... I didn't want to work and if I didn't have natural talent or quick improvements then I'd give up. Slowing down and eliminating that twitch made me accept and even enjoy the slower process. I'm not in a race. Anything high quality takes time to create, just like books and hand-made furniture.

I used to devour personal-development books that goaded me to hustle but then conversely said to enjoy the process. Totally mixed signals. I would envy people who seemed to hustle 24/7 but the "no sleep" attitude is not a quality life for me. Focusing on competing and beating others to the punch is a "lack" mentality – an assumption that there isn't enough to go around. Pushing hard day in and day out, and then burning out only to realize we didn't spend our time the way we wanted, is no life at all. That desperation of needing it now before someone else gets it will leave you empty, unfulfilled and burned out.

There is enough to go around.

Life is NOW.

Building a solid foundation is the key or our life will crumble. Health, knowledge, skills need to be curated.

Think of your daily life as an invitation-only opening at your carefully cultivated art gallery. The people that you invite to your opening are hand-selected, of similar interests and values, but diverse, including all ages, races and religions. The paintings you display reflect the beautiful possessions that you love and value. The performance artist's energy reflects the positive energy that you protect. The sculptures you choose represent the time and money you have invested in things you revere. Every day of your life can be a work of art. Celebrating, looking at, enjoying what you love, honor and value.

If your life is not carefully curated for you and by you, then you are living someone else's life.

> Approach life as a museum curator. They select the artwork and artifacts that best represents the story they want to convey. Everything is strategic and they exclude pieces that are pointless and detract from the beauty. The layout is organized for flow and clarity.
>
> For every decision you must ask yourself important questions.
>
> Relationships What kind of people do I want to be surrounded with? Do they love me, support me and respect me? Is this relationship reciprocal? Do I love, honor and respect them? Is this relationship hurting me or my family in some way?

Curation

Time How does this activity benefit me? Do I enjoy this? Do I love this or does this serve me in some way? The mindless scrolling or TV watching should stop. Choose what to look at and enjoy. Saying yes to events that you don't enjoy or serve you or your family should stop. Is this worthy of my time?

Goals Does this goal bring me joy or stress? Frustration or freedom? Is it meaningful? Your goals should reflect your life mission, values and purpose. Everything should build on your overall vision for life. Does this help create the life I want?

Thoughts Does this thought help or hurt me? Does thinking this way negatively affect how I feel? Am I feeding into fear and anxiety? Or am I building myself up? Our inner voice is evident in our daily choices and life. Thoughts become things and guiding and curating our thoughts will directly change (for the better) our life direction. I dismiss negative thoughts and only allow positive. There is not enough time for hurtful thoughts that slow and muddle the flow and clarity of our well-curated life.

07 Peace

Chaos vs. Calm.

I opened my eyes. The room was dark and dank. The paint was peeling, the thin mattress groaned as I pulled myself away from it. Stepping out onto the street in this Indian city led to an immediate assault on the senses. People on bikes, tuk tuks, in cars, piled on mopeds and on foot, all going to and fro while deftly avoiding the cows and garbage in the streets. Inhaling dust, spices and stench. I took a deep breath and trudged on. Horns blared, people yelled and dogs barked. Feelings of awe were peppered with anxiety. The streets of Mumbai and Varanasi were chaotic and beautiful in small doses. The experience was overwhelming to me, albeit interesting. My brain and body were in overdrive and totally depleted.

Chaos can be exhausting.

Conversely, when I stepped inside the gates of the Shechen Monastery in Bodh Gaya I immediately felt a sense of calm. The outside world was forgotten as I wandered the paths and watched the monks do their rituals and meditations. I felt safe, secure and happy. Outside the walls my senses were blasted, but inside them the simplicity brought peace.

The complexity of a fast city and new culture can be intoxicating. But like a Saturday night with too many Cuervo margaritas, too much dancing on the bar, too many trips to the bathroom to talk about boys and a too-loud bass, too much of a good thing is….too much. We all need a break from chaos, whether it's a Sunday spent all day in bed or a home that is a peaceful sanctuary from the traffic and demands of everyday life.

Simplicity is peace.

How can we use simplicity to create peace at home and in life?

Denmark has been rated the world's happiest country three times in the last few years. At first glance, you'll ask WHY? It's cold and dark for much of the year, the residents pay 40% of their income in taxes. How can they be so happy? The Happiness Institute has studied this extensively and potentially narrowed it down to one very crucial concept called hygge (pronounced hoo-gah). I've read books on this subject and I'll have some recommendations at the end of this book. For the sake of simplicity, I'll do my best to summarize this mindset that has infused a happy culture.

Happiness consists more in small conveniences or pleasures that occur every day, than in great pieces of good fortune that happen but seldom.

– Meik Wiking, "The Little Book of Hygge: Danish Secrets to Happy Living"

Hygge can be a noun, an adjective or a verb. If a home is hygge, it's warm, cozy, safe, quaint and simple. If you had a hyggely dinner it might have been a homemade pot roast with fresh baked bread and grass-fed butter. If you and your friends are going to the mountains to hygge… you'll probably sit under the stars and roast marshmallows by the campfire and swim in the lake during the day. Simple, natural, with good friends. Sounds that are hygge are soft music, thunderstorms, waterfalls and a crackling fire. To dive into this concept, I'll share some things that aren't hygge: big black tie affairs, Champagne and caviar, over-gifting, over-consumerism, stuffiness and pretentiousness.

Simplicity

While I may occasionally enjoy dressing up and sipping Champagne, I can appreciate the common thread woven throughout this way of living: simplicity. Simple, slow-cooked food made with love, deep conversation with friends, giving intentional gifts and not trying to impress other people. I dig it.

Denmark's neighbors, such as Sweden, are also forward-thinking regarding the environment, government and schooling. Why does Denmark beat them in the happiness factor? Because the Danes experience a deeper sense of security and trust. They also live with hygge intention… focusing on the simple pleasures of life which brings them peace, calm and joy.

On my journey to simplicity I've consciously focused on adopting a hygge way of living. Not only as a mindset shift but in the home. Lit candles, soft music, a variety of fabrics and more plants create a homey, warm atmosphere. I choose things in my home with a purpose… to make my sanctuary comfortable for me, my family and our guests. Everything is done with love and is meant to bring peace and relaxation.

If we hop in a plane and travel 5,300 miles and land in Japan and study the art of wabi-sabi, you'll see a unique but similar concept that also has the deep underlying theme of simplicity. Wabi-sabi is not only an aesthetic but a philosophy. It's about finding the beauty in things that are imperfect, modest, simple, humble and even unconventional. The Japanese studied nature and incorporated this wisdom into wabi-sabi. Many Japanese tea houses incorporate the principles of wabi-sabi. When you enter a true tea house, everyone is equal. The businessman and the store clerk, coming together over a cup of tea. The house is intimate yet imperfect. Modest but inviting. There is a deep-seated appreciation of the integrity of natural objects and processes.

When you walk in the woods and stare at awe at Mother Nature's creations, you don't wish that all the trees were alike and perfect. You relish the unique way each tree has grown and weathered through hundreds or thousands of storms over time. Nature is beautiful and imperfect and impermanent, which makes it that much more precious. If all trees were 6 feet, high, 2 feet around and exactly alike and never died, would you appreciate them? Would they be as beautiful?

One day as I was working in Key Largo on the beach, I looked up and saw a vulture land in a tree. My first reaction was disgust. But, I had wabi-sabi on the mind that day and so I looked closely at the long beak designed to dig out the carcasses of animals. Still, though, I asked,

"Where is the beauty?" But as I continued to study the bird, I noticed its beautiful shiny feathers in shades of blue and black. Seeing something beautiful in a typically grotesque creature shifted my mindset and I found myself filled with gratitude that it cleaned up the dead, rotting roadkill for us.

Some basic wabi-sabi principles:

- All things are impermanent and imperfect.
- Greatness is often in the overlooked details. When we rid ourselves of the distractions of life we can finally see the beauty in everything.
- Beauty can be seen in things that are ugly. The wabi-sabi philosophy is that beauty is a state of mind. If you are open to it, then you will see.
- Appreciate the cosmic order of things. The clay cracking and drying, the metal tarnishing and rusting make that object truly unique. One of a kind.
- Focus on intrinsic value vs. material flashiness. Like a Japanese tea room that is unpretentious, intimate, natural, irregular, earthy vs. an expensive nightclub that is snazzy, gaudy and ostentatious.

An unexpected benefit but imperative aspect of developing my simplicity mindset was acknowledging my imperfections. No, scratch that….embracing my imperfections. Ultimately removing the distractions helped me pause and reflect. Sometimes I didn't love what I saw but accepting me for me was a huge step in personal growth. Eliminating the outside influences helped me care less and seeing the beauty that was uniquely me... flaws and all...was freeing.

Get rid of all that is unnecessary. Wabi-sabi means treading lightly on the planet and knowing how to appreciate whatever is encountered, no matter how trifling, whenever it is encountered. In other words, wabi-sabi tells us to stop our preoccupation with success–wealth, status, power, and luxury–and enjoy the unencumbered life. Obviously, leading the simple wabi-sabi life requires some effort and will and also some tough decisions. Wabi-sabi acknowledges that just as it is important to know when to make choices, it is also important to know when not to make choices: to let things be. Even at the most austere level of material existence, we still live in a world of things.

Wabi-sabi is exactly about the delicate balance between the pleasure we get from things and the pleasure we get from freedom of things.

– Leonard Koren, "Wabi-Sabi: For Artists, Designers, Poets & Philosophers"

Simplicity

Simplicity and wabi-sabi are a state of grace and the words that come to mind are intelligent, heartfelt and modest.

Embracing simplicity at home, where our heart is, can be your state of grace recharge. We all have individual taste and to be attracted to a simple atmosphere isn't a black or white (rigid) rule of simplicity. It is true that if we had a chaotic, messy environment it leads to distraction and raised cortisol levels. Who wants additional unnecessary stress when you can just leave your house and fight traffic or turn on the news for a dose of premature-aging, heart-attack-inducing stress hormones.

Our homes are our sanctuary, the safe place where we rest, play and enjoy our family. Would you rather open the door to a zen-like spa or have a mountain of papers and clutter and toys to step over? You don't need a ton of money to create your personal sanctuary. It's simply eliminating unnecessary junk to create a calm atmosphere. Simply removing the "stuff," adding a couple 50 cent tea lights in recycled jam jars, having a few $2.99 herbs in a pot, turning the music on and maintaining a clean house can create the hygge and zen spa that brings you joy and peace.

Culling your house of duplicates, noisy toys and just-in-case items will have a profound effect on your happiness. I

Peace

was sick of organizing my crap so I got rid of 50% of it and never missed it! I only kept what brought me value or was truly needed. The more I got rid of, the lighter I felt. The kids played longer and I had more time to create. Yes, kids are still messy no matter what... but it was less daunting to clean when there was less to create that mess.

Simplicity is the ultimate form of sophistication.

– Leonardo da Vinci

08 Objects

I'm not evangelizing for living with nothing nor disapproving of material possessions. I like nice things and if something you have brings you joy, then enjoy! I drive an Audi and am grateful for its beauty.

But realize that I just don't care what you drive. I don't care about the square footage of your house. I'm not impressed that your cutting board cost $150. I care about you, what makes you truly happy, what makes you tick, what keeps you up at night.

Over-consumerism has permeated cultures all over the world. So many people are out there trying to impress others with "stuff." So many people filling the voids in their life with "stuff." But at the end of the day, what it is that we want? It is to be loved and valued.

What if we all shifted our consciousness and placed more value on thoughts, ideas and perspectives than on stuff? What if that retired couple took all that money they spent on stuff and spent it on something that would actually make them happy. Like giving to a charity, or experiences or maybe therapy? What if they stopped filling their void with things they don't want and focused their energy on growing as human beings? What if we all did that?

Any half-awake materialist well knows
— that which you hold holds you.

- Tom Robbins, "Still Life With Woodpecker"

Material possessions are necessary unless we want to move to a hut and live off the land. And anyone who knows me knows, that ain't happening! Sure, I'll hike the Adirondacks now and then, maybe even camp. One time I took a canoe out to a deserted island with friends and actually had to do ALL my business in the woods.

Day to day, though, I like quality. I like beauty. But I also like simplicity. My belongings don't define who I am. But a car is necessary so why not tell myself I'm worth a nice car? I'm ok with that. I often get complimented on my beautiful pair of pink Yves Saint Laurent shoes. At first I'd be embarrassed and say thank you and then justify it and tell them I got them secondhand (I did, I bought them off an app called Poshmark). I finally matured when it came

Objects

to receiving compliments. I sincerely say, "Thank you so much." I realized that I was judging myself and that that was my own baggage to work through. Just like we don't need to impress our neighbors and friends with flashy things, we also don't need to feel guilty about liking something of quality. Our possessions do not define us either way.

There are bookshelves lined with how-to's and self-help books about decluttering and minimalism. One of their common themes is to keep that which is necessary and sparks joy. I've implemented that in my life. There is a delicate balance between what sparks us joy and what we think sparks us joy. When you look at your house, open your closets and drawers and evaluate your purchases, ask yourself what your motivation behind each purchase was. The Louis Vuitton bag with all the trademark letters and brown leather….do you really love it? Or love what it represents? This can be difficult and eye-opening when we get to the heart of the matter. It is difficult to see that much of the money and time and energy of our life has gone into purchases that trick us into thinking we are one person, when we may not be.

We may be wooing neighbors with our $3000 back yard set, but we may also be wooing ourselves. And that is a tough pill to swallow. As I mentioned in the Mindset and

Growth chapters, when we adopt the simplicity mindset and shut out the constant influx of desperate data put out by advertising agencies we often see a creative and less materialistic person looking back at us. One that simply wants to be loved and valued for who they are. One that is worthy. Let me remind you... YOU are worthy because you are you, here on this beautiful planet.

Now that I'm a bit older and wiser, I can see through the beautifully staged and scripted stories we tell. I see my desperation to be loved mirrored back at me through others. We have been bombarded since birth by data from corporations and other humans. Marketing by companies saturated with greed and materialism, it's time to break the cycle.

But you do and I do. We can see through the beautifully staged and retouched photos on Instagram. The propaganda on TV. Going forward, we make decisions and purchases based on what we need and love and not what "they" want us to purchase. We live guilt- free for what we do love and no longer care what the neighbors think. Being rich isn't a bad thing. Being middle class isn't a bad thing. Being poor isn't a bad thing. We are all "we" and have more in common than we realize. Beautiful beings that want to be loved, cherished and valued. So, we can set out in the world and love, cherish and value others. Respect their time. Judge less. Take a moment to truly listen. Look at those we don't like and see that their so-called negative behaviors are mostly just cries for help.

When I was a child, I remember getting out of the car at my grandpa's and smelling the roses and seeing his beautiful hollyhocks. I gave Grandpa a big hug and he gave me a sweet piece of candy. We started our walk through his gardens. First stop, the vegetable garden where we snacked on fresh peas from the pod. My dad and he would talk about God knows what, and I would tune in and tune out, nodding my head occasionally but mostly just basking in the sunshine and the feel of the day. Feeling loved, enjoying the outside and the hygge moment. At the time hygge wasn't a part of my vocabulary but that's the closest way I can describe it as an adult. We wandered through his flower gardens, berry bushes, fruit trees. We chew on lemon balm and fresh peppermint. Talk to the neighboring cows, and listen to the birds. It was magical in every way. After that we'd go inside for lemonade and sit and chat or I'd go draw and color.

Going to my grandpas with my dad is one of my favorite childhood memories, those magical little moments of happiness with a distinct smell and feel and level of comfort. Most of my favorite memories did not involve an exorbitant amount of money. The most important factor was the people I was with – either myself alone, as I am my own best friend, or people I love and trust. The list of memories is long and wonderful: reading books, listening to my children's laughter, falling in love, coloring as a kid, having long dinners by the water, hiking and swimming in the Adirondacks, listening to the call of the loons (one of my favorite sounds of all time), taking taxis in NYC (the energy! the excitement!), staring in awe at the French Alps, feeling the butterflies in my belly when I'm struck with a great idea, eating chocolate.

I wish I could remember all the little moments in my life when I said, "I never want to forget this moment."

Sometimes I can't remember all the simple moments in life that I loved but I know my subconscious does. I know that the whole of my life is filled with many beautiful moments that create who I am and I know that those moments did not require "stuff.

09 Earth

Simplicity not only benefits us as individuals but as a society. Cutting out the crap and living a slightly more minimalistic lifestyle not only makes us happier (more on that in a bit) but cuts down on waste. A simpler lifestyle can help clean up this planet that is getting destroyed by landfills and global warming. Consumerism has enormous impacts on the environment and its sustainability.

Guangzhou, China. Shenzen, China.

Two cities paying the price for consumerism. They are close to drowning in the rising waters of the Pearl River Delta. Rushing to catch up to the demands of the world, China built a gargantuan industrial region with cities the size of nations, taking a huge toll on the environment and having a huge negative impact on global warming. In the 1980's these two cities had a little over 1 million people and now have 53 million people combined. They are growing fast but the multi-trillion dollar development is only 1 meter from the Pearl River. There is abundant evidence that global warming increases water levels, temperatures and the frequency of severe storms. The floods and storms in this area already overwhelm the neighborhoods but also threaten the world economy because of the immense amount of investments there. In 2016 rainfall was 16 percent above average and the summer floods cost $10 billion.

At first, the immense growth was welcomed by locals, who saw it as an opportunity to make more money. But the impact of the growth is changing many minds. The mangroves can no longer naturally protect the shore line so the sewage and filth is rising, garbage is trapped, the fish are killed off. Natural rivers and tributaries have been filled in for highways and office parks. Because 70% of Shenzen's mangroves are gone, the local authorities are going to add another twenty-one miles of landfill to the area. But landfill is not as effective as mangroves in handling storms.

This is just one small area of the world negatively affected by over-consumerism.

There is melting permafrost in Siberia; Mexico City is crumbling and thirsty; the Alps are losing tourism because they are warming three times more quickly than is the global average, and there has been a decades-long drought in Darfur. I could go on but I'm sure you can do your due diligence and find the massive burden we place on our beautiful planet. A London-based philanthropic group, Christian Aid, estimates that by 2050 floods, droughts, and famine caused by climate change will drive 250 million people from their homes. In contrast, only 5 million are estimated to be be refugees seeking asylum from persecution and only 50 million will be displaced due to extreme human rights violations.

But fixing over-consumption is complicated. As Richard Robbins, author of "Global Problems and the Culture of Capitalism," says, "Of the three factors environmentalists often point to as responsible for environmental pollution — population, technology, and consumption — consumption seems to get the least attention. One reason, no doubt, is that it may be the most difficult to change; our consumption patterns are so much a part of our lives that to change them would require a massive cultural overhaul, not to mention severe economic dislocation. A drop in demand for products, as economists note, brings on economic recession or even depression, along with massive unemployment."

So what do we do??

I know that global warming is massive, but each individual has a duty to do their own part. An individual's impact is admittedly tiny, but what if everyone made small positive changes every day? Consumed a little less, cooked at home more, walked or biked more, made fewer impulse buys?

I don't know the full economic answer to the question Robbins posed, but I do know this lifestyle isn't sustainable. If everyone made small positive changes and then focused on CREATING innovative ways to help the environment (urban planning, Elon Musk) that also still keep our economy afloat, then I know we'll be ok. If we recruit the collective conscious of millions of millions of people wanting to create true change, then I know without a doubt we can conquer the severe detrimental effects of global consumerism.

In fact, I know that such positive changes would not only help the earth, but making those changes is proven to make us happier! Not only that, but individual countries are now measuring happiness and seeing a growing dissatisfaction with the destructive impact of economic growth on the environment. Material affluence is no longer an accurate measure of happiness and quality of life. Per the Sustainable Happiness study "To have happy and fulfilling lives actually requires more than increasing GDP or larger paychecks at the end of the month."

This change is a paradigm shift that is happening throughout the world. The GDP is slowly losing its higher-than-God status and we are ready to clean up the industrial era's toxic leftovers and evolve.

The dissatisfaction, dis-ease and distaste for the glut of overconsumption is fuel for our human evolution to put well-being at the forefront of our goals and policies.

Happiness is neither a frivolity nor a luxury. It is a deep-seated yearning shared by all members of the human family. It should be denied to no one and available to all.

– Ban Ki-moon,
Former Secretary-General, United Nations

So how does sustainability and "saving the earth" increase happiness? I'm so glad you asked, my dear friend! The Happiness Institute study shows that sustainable behavior and waste prevention actually BOOST positive feelings. Can people feel good about efficiently managing waste and living simpler?

Yep.

The study in a nutshell: People reusing things= happier. People reducing garbage = happier. People buying products in refillable packages = happier.

Happiness Institute study: "Happiness is nothing without sustainability – and the other way around. As such, they aim at the same goal: advancing human well-being and enhancing quality of life."

For humans to be truly happy, we've found that it is very important to feel that we are part of something bigger than ourselves. We all want to belong to a tribe of sorts.

Even though there have been multiple studies done, we are just on the cusp of understanding this. It seem people choose to live with simplicity because they feel more autonomous, competent, and socially related. Simplicity increases self-reliance. Also, our brains are hardwired to produce a sense of pleasure and well-being when we engage in activities that ensure the survival of the individual and the species. We are also rewarded in our sense of well-being by helping others, the so-called "helper's high."

I'm not here to be judgey about how much you consume or how much waste you create. I just want to share the global impact of consumerism and the sense of

Earth

community that is created when we all pitch in and do a little bit to save the earth. I still purchase things I don't always need, I still create garbage and try as I might... I still have some plastic in my house. No one is perfect but little steps in consuming and wasting less can have a humongous impact on our well-being.

10 Intention

I was sitting on a folding chair with a paper cup of fruit punch having small talk with a friend of a friend's aunt. She was nice enough, but small talk is not my thing so I excused myself to grab a bite. Macaroni salad, baked ziti, tomato pie all piled my plate. The standard fare of an upstate New York bridal shower. All was ok, tolerable until the games started. OMG please make it stop. I hid in the bathroom for a while. Poured myself more punch. And then endured another hour of opening presents until I made my escape, all the while asking myself "WHY? Why did I say yes?"

Why do we say yes to things we don't enjoy or want to do? I guess we don't want to seem like jerks. There is a deep fear that I have of seeming unfun if I say no to things. But so much valuable time, energy and money have gone into making other people happy in my life that it was time to say enough is enough.

As I embraced simplicity, lived a life that was more authentically me, and curated my intentional life, I have

Simplicity

learned when to say no and when to say yes to obligations. I essentially "decluttered" my mind, which I would say is more important than cleaning out my closets.

How many of us say yes to things we do not enjoy? Events, jobs, meetings that bring us nothing but stress. Learning the art of a polite "no thank you" can clear you of the dreaded obligation and the guilt that piles up regarding it. Oh, I wish I knew how to be more discerning with my time when I was younger; I think of the wasted energy I put into things. The stress beforehand of trying to think of an excuse, or the lie of an excuse and the guilt that preceded and succeeded that lie. The pure boredom of said event or the money that went into the gift, the tickets, the gas. The time given up worrying about it and then enduring it. All of that did NOT need to happen.

"Beware the barrenness of a busy life"

– Socrates

As a recovering people pleaser, I'd never want to offend anyone by telling them their cookie exchange is just not my thing. I'm more of a jump out of airplanes or curl up with a good book kind of girl. I have an allergy to small talk, forced events or anything remotely crafty. I do think it's an amazing accomplishment that you finished your Master's degree at 33, or that you are having a baby (I love babies, anyone can tell you that, and I've had two of my own) or that you are celebrating a promotion. I applaud and love you for these things…but the events that go along with them are so not me.

We all have things in our life that we do when we do not want to. Think of the time, money and energy you have devoted to volunteering or committees or whatever it may be. We all owe it to ourselves to be "us." To live with intention means to say yes or no to something and not blindly follow the pack. FOMO (fear of missing out), be gone.

Valuing our time, money and energy with intention takes work but will mean a simpler, happier life. Choosing whom we spend time with and how we spend our time intentionally is what makes our life a work of art.

The foundation of living with simplicity is intentional living. Ridding myself of mindless pacifiers was the first step. Now, intention permeates everything I do, say, buy and spend my energy on. I culled every item in my house, keeping only the ones that were useful or we loved as a family. I stopped the trips to stores to mindlessly buy things that met my eye that day but in the long run I didn't enjoy or value. The clothes I purchase, I now think about and examine. Is it good quality? Do I love it? Will it be useful? Yes, I buy more expensive items but now I save money by not purchasing throwaway clothes or making impulse buys. I no longer spend money frivolously on a quick boost of adrenaline. I'd rather take that money and spend it on an experience instead of a material thing.

Everyone is different. There is no right or wrong way to live intentionally. Knowing yourself and what you value will help you make decisions and shape your life in the way you want.

The people in my life are cultivated intentionally.

How I spend my day is intentional. Everything I do is either necessary to live and function as an adult or honors my core values and priorities. I ask myself... what's best for my health? My family? Happiness? Growth? Creativity? My business? Learning to say no to time suckers, negativity or things that will stress me or my family out has been imperative. We do not overbook ourselves. Cutting out the extra bull leaves time to do things I love like write, draw, read, spend time with family, practice tennis, take spontaneous road trips and enjoy nature.

Why live with intention? It decreases stress, and knowing when to say yes or no ultimately brought me happiness, health, and freedom. I live life by my own terms, spending time with those who lift me up, challenge me and accept me for who I am.

> *"Intentional living is the art of making our own choices before others' choices make us."*
>
> – Richie Norton,
> *"The Power Of Starting Something Stupid"*

A shift happens when you live like this. The simple things in life become sweeter. Sipping my coffee instead of slurping it allow me to thoroughly enjoy it. I can be fully present with my children instead of stressed or distracted.

Another unexpected thing happened as I've embarked on my simplicity journey. I have less fear. Ridding myself of perceived societal expectations, peer pressure and "keeping up with the Joneses" was freeing. Also, this journey has allowed me to fully get to know myself more than at any other time in my life.

When we are true to the core of ourselves and honor our values and do activities that are congruent with our

Simplicity

essence, then we become unstoppable. The fight and resistance is over. That battle of our trueness and outside influence fizzles out. I no longer question my decisions. I listen to my gut first and I let go of trying to control everything. I feel more in tune to my intuition now more than ever. My inner wisdom leads me (and it may at times lead me to the right person as a mentor... I don't have all the answers but I can find them). I just don't worry. I trust. I do have roadblocks and bumps in the road but they're less stressful than before I started this journey. I know that they are part of life and I ask myself what good will come of this? What does this mean? What is the reason this happened?

Then I let it go.

The answer always comes to me. Always. The better path is illuminated in my mind or a new idea pops into my head. The answer is always revealed when I ask because I trust myself, I've eliminated distractions and outside influences on big decisions.

As I mentioned, I do still have selected mentors and friends whom I can turn to. I bounce ideas off and spend time with people I love and respect. We learn, grow, challenge and enjoy each other. But when it comes to big decisions, I listen to myself even if they have an intelligent opposite perspective. I value their insight but go with my heart.

* * *

My Evolution in Living With Intention: 4 Decades in 4 Paragraphs

Decade 1: 0-10
I was a child of the 80's, watching cartoons only on Saturday mornings. Otherwise I was playing with dolls, reading, drawing or playing outside.

Decade 2: Ages 10-20
Boys, school, teenage angst, confusion. Who am I? I thought someday I'd make $50,000 a year and be rich and secure. Started this decade a child and ended it in college.

Decade 3: Ages 20-30
Consuming and creating and still finding myself. Societal expectations played a major role in my decisions. I chose nursing as a career even though writing or acting was what I wanted to do. I married the wrong person. I traveled the world looking for my identity. I was a yuppie, hippie, partier, introvert, extrovert, reader. I was outdoorsy and I was fancy. So many hats in my 20's!

Decade 4: Ages 30-40

Increased confidence. I owned a business in Costa Rica, did graphic design, was a health and fitness coach and a nurse manager. I was slightly minimalistic but still consuming. I made more money than ever but was always dissatisfied with the amount. I had children, life slowed down. Then I had health issues that forced me to pause and reflect, leading to my still-ongoing metamorphosis into living with intention, as described below.

Now: More confidence than ever. Slower, simpler living, intentional actions and decisions, creating vs. consuming, less STUFF, children growing and enjoying the moment. I feel simple, intentional, authentic, fulfilled, happy, secure. I stopped doing things that were not congruent with me.

11 Authenticity

The truth hurts:

After the heartbreak of a short-lived marriage I bought a one way ticket to Ireland. I was running from the pain but trying to remember who I was before I became this broken soul. I had big questions and thought I could find the answers on my journey, that they would just present themselves in the dusty books I grabbed from each used bookstore I spent hours in.

A few weeks after landing in Shannon I found myself in a flat in Galway with an Irish roommate. Each day I aimlessly roamed and burned through money in markets, bookstores and fancy restaurants where I'd sit for hours reading and journaling and watching people walk by. "Sharon" offered me a job at a little cafe in Doolin (near the Cliffs of Moher). After years of ICU nursing I became a waitress and a crappy barista in her little art cafe. It baffled me that I could professionally care for a patient who was intubated and had a dozen drips, a swan catheter, CRRT, and septic shock, but I could not make a damn cup of coffee.

I stayed at Sharon's mother's house, which was extremely kind of her because I was technically a stranger. I passed judgment on this woman, though. She was in her late 50's and dating a man in his 20's, which at the time I thought was so odd. Her house was a mess and after she told me she cleaned the sheets for me and showed me the room I was to sleep in, I pulled back the covers to find hair and the stench of another human there before me. I'd say those sheets hadn't been washed in months. She and her boyfriend would stay up partying until the wee hours each and every night.

I decided to leave Ireland after a few months. Ultimately, I was still searching for me and the answers were not here. When I was leaving she told me, "Gretchen, you've got a long way to go. I hope you find yourself in your travels. Good luck."

I smiled but I was seething inside. Oh, she made me so mad! How dare she?

At the time I felt so shocked that she would judge me when she lived the way she did. I didn't actually get it until years later. She was not judging me, merely stating a fact. I was lost. And she was unapologetically, authentically herself and she did not give a shit what other people thought. I cared way too much what people thought at the

Authenticity

age of 28. I internalized her comment as a critique instead of recognizing the sage advice of a woman who had lived many years more than me. She was flawed but 100% herself. She was authentic and I was still consumed with fears and self-doubt. I still cared way too much what other people think.

> *There is a voice inside of you*
> *that whispers all day long,*
> *"I feel that this is right for me,*
> *I know that this is wrong."*
> *No teacher, preacher, parent, friend*
> *or wise man can decide*
> *what's right for you - just listen to*
> *the voice that speaks inside.*
>
> – Shel Silverstein

I was addicted to approval. I desperately needed Sharon's mother to like me and her stating a fact about myself that I was trying to hide ticked me off. The truth hurts.

It's time to break the approval addiction that most of us have. Seeking someone else's approval and basing our life around someone else's opinion is one of the most debilitating of human afflictions. By eliminating the desperate need to be approved of, we can expand/ elevate our existence by truly being US.

While Sharon's mother was merely stating a fact that hurt, many of us fuel all of our actions by seeking the approval of others. And most of the time it's their tainted opinions that control our actions. They've got their own bag of pain that shouldn't influence what we choose to do in life.

Your happiness shouldn't derive from the fear-based opinions of those riddled with self-limiting beliefs on joy, love and abundance. Never give up your hopes and dreams to the negativity that weak people spew. Instead, use your real world experience and your gut to lead you to your joy.

Authenticity is correlated with many aspects of psychological well-being, including vitality, self-esteem, and coping skills. Acting in accordance with one's core self—a trait called self-determination—is ranked by some experts as one of three basic psychological needs, along with competence and a sense of relatedness.

Some experts ranked authenticity as one of three basic psychological needs, along with competence and a sense of relatedness. It's something we all hunger for at every age. Authenticity is self-awareness. Its key traits are iden-

Authenticity

tifying our strengths and weaknesses, acting in synch with our beliefs no matter what, and having a strong sense of self-worth and purpose, confidence in mastering challenges, and the ability to follow through in pursuing goals.

Living authentically is not for the faint of heart, though. Making conscious, hard choices day in and day out can be hard when it seems it's easier to follow the crowd or blend in. Being our authentic self means admitting we are flawed and messy human beings, and in our perfectionist society that admission is scary to some.

But I ask, what is our life if we are living it for someone else? To realize our full potential and to discover our unique individuality, the Bhagavad Gita suggests you have to "discern your own highly idiosyncratic gifts, and your own highly idiosyncratic calling."

To live a truly authentic life you have to know who you are and have the guts to be you. That is a twofold task. The first part, knowing yourself, comes from spending time with yourself without the pacifiers and distractions. Some people meditate but you don't have to get fancy unless you want to. Simply let yourself THINK, get bored and ask yourself important questions like WHY? WHAT? WHO? WHEN? Then let go and open your ears to what your inner wisdom has to say.

Simplicity

The quieter you become, the more you can hear.

– Ram Dass

Having the guts to show yourself to the world is the second requirement for an authentic life. It was not an overnight transformation for me, but nothing worthwhile is. The less I cared about outside influence, the less overall fear I had. When decisions felt right (in my soul) and were congruent with me, then they were easier. When I felt resistance, I re-evaluated. Many times the resistance was fear of vulnerability. It's instinctual to avoid situations where we might get hurt. Not only is it our brains protecting us, but our past relationships influence our present-day decisions.

Surrounding ourselves with authentic people can also give us the courage to be our true selves. Authentic people are fallible and flawed, but we feel good just being around them. We feel safe around authenticity, we know they don't have an agenda and are generally trustworthy (we can all fall short of this at times). Nobody is perfect but we can all be authentically us.

Living inauthentically is a lie. Many of us lie to ourselves and to the people around us when we don't honestly show

Authenticity

ourselves to the world. Not only can living with simplicity help us discover our authentic self but living authentically can help simplify our lives. No longer will we have to live with the burden of a lie. Our relationships will flourish and become deeper and more meaningful. We'll also weed out the superficial people in our lives that hold us back from sharing our beautiful light with the world. We gain power with our authenticity.

You are not what you do, who you love, what you have, you are YOU underneath it all. Your power comes from tapping into and accepting and loving that you are unique. Once you really know this, you'll never be superfluous ever again.

Living inauthentically doesn't mean we are hiding all the "bad" parts of our personality. Sometimes we hide our passions or don't acknowledge and share our strengths. Sometimes we dull our light around others to make them feel comfortable.

Being overbearing, loud and in your face doesn't necessarily mean authenticity either. Some hide behind the facade of shoving opinions down someone's throat. It's about being REAL.

When you go through the pain and process of removing the mask, you finally see you in the mirror. The real you.

The authentic you. The gloriously flawed you. When you release YOU from the chains you bound yourself with, then life will happen. Amazing things that you never even imagined!

After emerging from my cocoon and living with complete and utter authenticity, I found that life was easy, free, happy. Not without bumps as I mentioned, but just smoother. That's when the magic started to happen.

> *"My life is my message"*
>
> *– Gandhi*

The first dose of real magic I experienced was a month or so after I opened my publishing company and as I was writing this book. I had another book I was co-authoring in the works, but nothing published yet other than my "Joy Manifesto." I had a children's series written but not published. I really felt like I had made a shift and was excited about the process but nothing to "show" yet. I wasn't even ready to take on clients yet with my publishing company. One day I opened my email and found what at first I thought was spam. It was from a woman who said she was a "fan," knew of my "Joy Manifesto" and would love it

Authenticity

if I would speak to 11,000 women at The Massachusetts Conference For Women (nonprofit women's empowerment conference with Gloria Steinem, Meryl Streep and so many more powerful women). Tears rolled down my face and I was a bit perplexed. Was this a mistake? I cried an ugly albeit happy cry as I called my husband. This was a huge honor with other powerful, compassionate women leaders. I wondered how I could even be considered? I wanted to ask her "Why me?" but didn't want to break the spell. It didn't feel real until I was on their website with my bio.

Other amazing things like this started happening to me that blew my mind. I didn't ask, the Universe provided. I didn't feel like I needed validation that I was on the right path (most of my life I sought validation) but this giant bear hug from God showed me that being ME and following my dreams was ultimately the best choice I've ever made (besides having children of course). The magic of being you will reveal itself when you least expect it, but expect it. Because when you allow the world to see YOU, you stop resisting what is meant to be. You serve the world by showing your true colors. You empower the world by allowing us to see your beauty and flaws. You show the children of the world that they are ok and loved just the way they are. You give them the courage by setting the example and paving the way. Individual reformation precludes social reformation.

Simplicity

Ask yourself, "If people knew the real me they'd know_____."

There are mountains of books, lectures, videos about HOW to be authentic and find yourself, create yourself. You can study religion, philosophy and psychology. But as you have found throughout this book, it doesn't have to be complicated. You knew who you were at age 4. You felt you were strong and talented and capable. Slowly, society, peers and well meaning (or not so well meaning) parents, all started to affect how you thought about yourself. Your story. Now it's time to strip away their opinions and find that artist, or engineer, or author, and be THAT person, just a little older and wiser and full of life experience.

Authenticity takes courage. Honesty. Vulnerability. The very young and very old are good at being themselves, but what about the middle? Why can't we master being ourselves like a child so easily does?

Our deepest fear is not that we are inadequate. Our deepest fear is that we are powerful beyond measure. It is our light, not our darkness that most frightens us. We ask ourselves, Who am I to be brilliant, gorgeous, talented, fabulous? Actually, who are you not to be? You are a child of God. Your playing small does not serve the world. There's

Authenticity

nothing enlightened about shrinking so that other people won't feel insecure around you. We are all meant to shine, as children do. We were born to make manifest the glory of God that is within us. It's not just in some of us; it's in everyone. And as we let our own light shine, we unconsciously give other people permission to do the same. As we're liberated from our own fear, our presence automatically liberates others.

– Marianne Williamson, New York Times bestselling author of "A Return to Love" and many more books

When we are ready to show the world our authentic selves, it can be particularly daunting when our true self is very different than the facade we created over the course of our lifetime. This is where it takes courage and intellectual honesty to boldly reveal the truth. The truth always sets you free. In life, the most respected and loved people were always the ones who admitted flaws and mistakes, learned and grew from them and shared that with the people they loved. There is not a single person in the world who hasn't distorted the truth in one way, shape or form. But how we address that mistake is what separates us from ordinary, average. The more we are US, the more we elevate our very existence.

12 Freedom

free·dom
ˈfrēdəm/

Noun
1. the power or right to act, speak, or think as one wants without hindrance or restraint.
2. the absence of necessity, coercion, or constraint in choice or action
3. liberation from slavery or restraint or from the power of another

Today is a Tuesday. It's 9:30 a.m. and I'm sitting in bed, working on this chapter as I drink my mushroom coffee. It's summer break, no school for the kiddos. We went out to a long dinner and were all up late last night, so they are sleeping in. I don't make to-do lists anymore but I do have three goals for today. Other than that, no agenda, no stress, no expectations.

I don't always live a life of leisure, but since Simplicity and I have grown tight, I've embraced freedom and every

Simplicity

second of my day is impacted. Simplicity didn't change me, but it freed me. I'm still me, just liberated. I have less worry, less anxiety, less stress. My shoulders are light.

Freedoms you can obtain from embracing Simplicity:

- Worrying about timelines. I get my daughter to school on time, make my appointments and get to the plane on time, and otherwise I'm chill. If you are rushing and stressed, ask yourself "What's the worst that can happen?"
- Writing long to-do lists. Forget that, it doesn't bring me joy. I focus on one thing at a time.
- Sweating the small stuff. In the grand scheme of things, does it really matter?
- Mindlessly saying yes. Infusing intention into every action will free you from compulsively saying yes when you mean no.
- Not showing the world who you really are. Never dull your light to make someone feel better about themselves. You are now officially free to be YOU.
- Collecting too much stuff. Hoarding is stressful, even if it's organized chaos. Let it go.

It may be that the human race is not ready for freedom. The air of liberty may be too rarefied for us to breathe. Certainly I wouldn't be writing this book, on this subject, if living with freedom were easy. The paradox seems to be, as Socrates demonstrated long ago, that the truly free individual is free only to the extent of his own self-mastery. While those who will not govern themselves are condemned to find masters to govern over them.

– Steven Pressfield, "War of Art"

I spent this book telling you how easy Simplicity is and then add this quote. Why? Because it's a paradox. Considering myself, I'm an American, I'm educated, I'm healthy, I have a wonderful family and a certain level of affluence but yet, I struggled with allowing myself to be free. To go against the grain and stand out from the crowd. To overcome self-doubt and grow my self confidence. To have the courage to be vulnerable and real. Being free means not doing what everyone else is doing and that can be scary at first.

I had the hardest time sitting down to write this chapter. Because it's the most important and I worried how to convey my message with words. How can I find them? How can I show you the importance of freedom and empower you to take control? I don't want to fail you. What story of mine will be compelling enough to inspire you to take action?

I'm not sure I have a single compelling story but I can tell you of many little stories when I had the most freedom in my life and felt ALIVE, empowered and happy. That February in 2002 when I moved to midtown Manhattan and worked at St. Vincent's Hospital (now closed) in Greenwich Village: I felt like Mary Tyler Moore throwing up my hat every day getting on the subway to go to work. The pulse and energy of the city filled me. I felt so grown up, happy and FREEEEE! Or that time I packed up my life and bought a one-way ticket to Ireland to lick my wounds after a broken relationship. I explored Europe and lived on my own terms: FREE! Or, that time when I filled my purse with money and flew down to Costa Rica and bought a business, I was challenged but FREE. Especially living in another country, I had the opportunity to completely be me and totally FREE.

Each time I reinvented myself and followed my heart I experience my definition of freedom. Conquering fears, having the courage to do what I love and the strength to be the me of the moment has been incredibly empowering and joy-inducing.

What would it take for you to find your freedom? Ask yourself, do you want to govern yourself? Or to be governed?

To sum up this book in one sentence: Look at every action you take and ask yourself, "Why am I doing this?"

Simplicity is not about rules or restraint. It's making art out of living. You are able to have and do less, while gaining richer insight and experiences. It's a state of being conscious and aware, allowing you to be present in your life.

Human nature predisposes us to wanting more. We constantly seek because we want to eliminate the desire, we want to stop wanting and just be. That calmness and peace can be attained without the pain of wanting by adopting a Simplicity mindset. With Simplicity, we use intention to get to the root of our actions and desires. The beauty of letting go is that life becomes less complex and we become free to be ourselves. Life falls into place as it should.

In the modern age we are constantly bombarded by advertisements, highlight reels of other people's daily lives, and an abundance of life "filters" which causes us to overcomplicate things and live in fear and lack. When we start living with Simplicity we are able to shut out the noise and finally hear ourselves think. We achieve breakthroughs and a peace that cannot be bought or achieved with the next promotion.

Simplicity is not about taking away things that you love. This is not a how-to book but rather, a fluid mindset philosophy. We each define what is important to ourselves, so every single one of us will have a different journey and outcome.

This section of the book is a bit misleading, as there is no way I can tell you how to live your life. What I can do is inspire you to choose your actions, belongings and thoughts with intention. You choose what to focus on and what to cull from your life.

Bye, For Now

Every day for the last two months, just as I finishing up this book, I woke up with a gorilla on my chest. My breath was shallow to accommodate his weight. I had to get up and sling him over my shoulders and walk through each day doing the Fireman's Carry with my burden. I tried to bury my head in the sand to hide from him but he mocked me while sitting on my back. I could not escape. You see, I got lost in my own journey. In September 2017 I had a health setback (more to come on health and vitality in a future book) and got behind in doing my work.

Then, I couldn't do my work.

I started overthinking, comparing, becoming over-critical of myself and indecisive about how to conclude this book. I started to give up on myself. Instead of getting back to the basics and living with Simplicity, I defaulted to complexity and stress because of a bump in the road. I lost my stride. I missed my self-imposed deadlines. I was humbled. My goal was to have this completed for a that

Simplicity

huge speaking gig in Boston I mentioned earlier, the one with Gloria Steinem, Meryl Streep and 11,000 women in attendance. But guess what? It won't be completed. I still have to go to this event and stand strong, though. Do you know how badly I wanted to cancel? How hard I fell into the trap of perfectionism and self-sabotage? I was one click away from emailing the organizer of the Massachusetts Conference for Women and saying I was still too "sick" to attend.

But I didn't.

It's 3 weeks away and I will go with my head held high. Humbled and with a story to tell. I'm human and afraid of failure as well as afraid of success, but I'm going for it anyway.

How did I finally get my gorilla off my chest? I got back to the basics and re-read my book. I shut out the inner negative dialogue. I worked on taking baby steps each day. I meditated. I went on my Joy of Living Retreat not as a leader, but as an attendee with everyone that signed up with me. I went for walks and reconnected with nature. I found gratitude in the simplest of things. I stopped worrying about becoming a "bestselling author" and missing my one opportunity. No, the universe is abundant and this one conference does not determine my value.

Bye, For Now

Learn from my mistakes and know that we all falter in our life's journey. But keeping the Simplicity mindset or revisiting it in a time of need will never let you down.

Letters Of Triumph

I asked a few friends and fans to submit letters sharing their stories of overwhelm and simplicity mindset. Here are a few to read for inspiration:

Read this letter from Olivia about attachment to and detachment from "stuff":

When I moved from one state to another I spent many hours contemplating whether or not to take all the "stuff" I owned with me. My choices were to rent a vehicle, pack, haul, and unpack what was essentially a house full of belongings or sell, donate, and recycle most of it and start with a clean slate. I spent so much time considering my options because I felt I was attached to so many of the things I owned. I loved my big comfortable couch. And I'd spent hours and many trips to furniture stores to pick out my bedroom set.

I chose, with much trepidation, to shed my belongings and I moved with only what fit into my small SUV. I drove with a vehicle full of well-packed items, wondering how soon I'd start missing items I'd discarded. Upon arrival in my new state I found a freedom that was indescribable and unexpected. I had little to unpack and I felt suddenly lighter, less burdened by the things I owned. I did need to purchase a few small furniture items for storage but even this felt light and uncluttered.

Several years later, with an apartment now comfortably stuffed, I often reflect on that found freedom and yearn to unload what is not necessary. If I were not pursuing a professional career, paring down would be an even simpler task, but I find that I am no longer "attached" to things I own. And I do not crave more, only what I find necessary to be competitive in my chosen field. I tend to keep things now based on sentimental value, not monetary value.

***

From Nicole, about intention and focus during a divorce:

It's a Wednesday morning. I'm off work, the sun couldn't be brighter, the trees and grass are a lively shade of green, my beautiful daughters are crawling out of bed with smiles on their faces and we have the entire day to spend together doing whatever our hearts desire. Perfection. Right?

No. Entering the process of a divorce after 12 years of marriage is daunting. At times my life seems to be spiraling out of control. Days that should be the epitome of perfection instead leave me feeling lost, confused, full of uncertainty and anxiety. To top off this less than desirable state of mind, I also feel like I've lost who I am – my love of nutrition, prepping healthy meals for my family, working out, continually learning, new exercises. I've lost it all. The desire just isn't there. Some days it even feels like a chore to be a good mom. One who isn't snippy, mean and on edge. I can be consumed by the bad and too easily allow it to drown out everything in my life that is good. Overall, a lost sense of identity. Who am I if I don't have the desire or motivation for things I once was passionate about?

A self-help junky, I started reading, listening and writing down everything I thought may help me regain control. I had the tools, tactics and most of the know-how, but continued to struggle. I listened to a podcast, "The Science on Motivation," in which Lenny Wiersma explained that you don't need to be motivated to get started. You simply start with doing! He said, "How long are you going to feel sorry for yourself?" That was it. I was feeling such self-pity, I couldn't get past the fact that I was my own cure. But the key was fixing it, not just understanding it. I've discovered that the days I start with true intention bring joy, calm, gratification, happiness and satisfaction.

Simplicity

Conversely, I've found those days which are done haphazardly bring stress, anger, anxiety and fear. This was my key - to ensure I go after each day with intent. Intent to be happy. Intent to be an inspiration. Intent to work out. Intent to seek my passions. Intent to eat nutritious food. Intent to be positive. Intent to be a patient mom. Intent to tell myself I was going to be okay! Waking in the morning and intentionally planning to include joy, positivity and working towards a purpose - I have found myself in a much better place. The certainty of routine and autopilot may feel like what you need, but I believe that it must contain intent to be productive. In doing this, you starve your distractions and feed your focus!

* * *

From Tonya, about her hidden talent for jewelry-making:

When my creative side began to show about nine years ago, I was a little overwhelmed at first. But my idea to stay home and take care of our 3rd child, with whom I was pregnant at the time, turned out to be a blessing in disguise. This led to me opening my own shop on Etsy. The idea just came to me like a bolt of lightning and I acted on it. Everything was falling into place for me, from the article in the magazine at the doctor's office talking about Etsy and how you can sell your crafts, to all the business advice that was just flowing to me. It was all there and I went with it. I then spent countless hours planning and putting it all into action. Making my unique wedding bouquets was the start of it all.

Once I got the shop set up and the business license, I finally began creating. The ideas would flow to me like an endless river even to the point of being woken up with ideas. It was something that I could not turn off. I created piece after unique piece. My ideas were a bit different from your traditional items, and I like that I was making things you did not normally see, and that is how I created my own personal style. It was a part of me and I was sharing that with the world.

When it was time to start listing I will admit I was terrified at first. The doubt creeped in, and the negative thoughts started to take hold. Thoughts like: "Will people like my stuff?" to "You will never be able to do this." I pushed through it and didn't listen to any of it. Once I got my items up there and orders came in, I was even more terrified. I was really putting myself out there at this point and there was no turning back. This whole creating side of me was very new. It had been lying dormant for so long and once I unleashed it I could not stop at all. It definitely was a whirlwind of uncertainty of the unknown.

Simplicity

Since I have been doing this my creative side has revealed so much to me. I have let this part of me shine and I have expanded to making unique jewelry as well. My second shop on Etsy just opened up a few months ago. I am still working on all of it. The biggest thing that this has taught me is to share your gifts with the world. You were given these talents for a reason, whatever they are to you. Mine didn't show itself till I was much older, but now that I overcame my fear of sharing that aspect of me with the world, I realize it is something that I would not change about me. It has made me more confident in myself and my abilities, especially as a woman, a mother and a wife. Everything from obtaining the business knowledge to opening my shop was all done by me and it taught me I can do anything. I can say now since I have traveled down this road that I am very comfortable being creative. It has taught me so much.

* * *

From Jessie, about FOMO and happiness:

Everyone wants to be happy. Ultimately, you are responsible for your own happiness. Your spouse, loved ones, family members, and friends are not responsible for making you happy. You have to figure out what makes you happy and do it. If you keep waiting on others to make you happy you will just keep getting disappointed. Because we all feel a little self-entitlement. Such as, "Well, I am a single mom and I don't have two incomes and can't ever have a boat or go on any big fun trips. The people who do have two incomes should invite me." You will feel disappointed every time you don't get invited. Instead what I have learned is look at what you do have. How can you help someone else out? Here is a thought: You look on someone as less fortunate than you, but to someone else, you are their less fortunate.

I have FOMO (Fear of Missing Out), thus making it very difficult to say no when asked to do something. Thus making my life super busy and stressful. When I see something is happening and I am not a part of it I feel that I missed out on something amazing. Over the years I have found that most of the times it was not the amazing thing that I thought it would be. With always contemplating if I should go or miss out, I realized that I am making my life too complex and too stressful. It is ok to say, "Thank you, but this time I am going to pass," or "Thanks for the offer." Yes, I potentially missed out on something but I became less stressed and less tired by not always saying yes, thus making me a happier person.

After having my first-born I have learned what simplicity really means. For me it means waking up and singing to my baby, talking to her, and just enjoying every minute I get with her. Don't get me wrong. There are times that it is very hard to just chill and live in the moment. I love to have everything planned and, you see, that is not how parenting works. Learning to live more "simply," not planning, has made me a happier mom, wife, daughter, sister, co-worker and person.

When I find myself getting unhappy about a person or situation I step back and ask myself, "Why are you unhappy?" The situation? Communication? Event? Timing? Most of the time I find that it is something that I did not clearly communicate, thus making the outcome less than desirable. If I had clearly communicated I would not have been unhappy.

Sometimes you have to sacrifice your happiness to make others happy. I find most of the time when I think I am sacrificing my happiness by make someone else happy I am greatly mistaken. Taking part in others' happiness will always make you happy.

The key to true happiness is being grateful for your key components and finding the blessings in your life. The key components in life: health, food, clothes, and shelter. Yes it is that simple. Be happy.

Letters of Triumph

***

From Carrie to herself:

Dear Self,

It's time to remember you're a grown-up and grow up.

Why was it difficult to find contentment when I received everything I wanted? I met my husband, who is my best friend. We got married. We bought a beautiful home together, which others have not been able to do. We got pregnant easily with twins as I watched dear friends and family struggle with infertility and miscarriage. My career moved steadily along. I had everything I wanted.

But I still didn't feel content. How could that be? I was riddled with anxiety attacks, insecurities and second-guessed most decisions. My husband noted that my anxiety was almost unbearable on Sundays as I prepared for my week. He loved me but didn't understand so he would just stay clear as I tried to handle my anxiety. Family members suggested medication but I was determined that I had to deal with it behaviorally and not through medication. Medication would not take away the why of feeling this way. Medication would not help my brain figure out how to cope. But all my formal education

Simplicity

did not teach me about how to figure this out. I was so overwhelmed I would shut down. I was tired, worried and more insecure than ever.

Then I remembered that... I'm a grown-up... and I grew up. None of this just happened to me. I chose every single thing. I did. It was only me to make me content. It was not the role of my husband, children, career or home to make me happy. So I simplified.

I changed jobs for work/life balance. We cut out cable television and sold or donated everything that was extra, everything that was in the "I might need or use that one day" category. I don't notice the television we don't watch, or miss the clutter taking up space. I went back to cooking to save money and to monitor what my children ate, which saved money, but made us healthier and made me fall back in love with cooking so much that we grow a lot of our own vegetables and herbs for the summer and fall.

Most importantly I prioritized my time for myself, my husband, my children and my career. In that order. I take time for me so I can be the best for the other three priorities. Next is the relationship with my husband as we lay the foundation for our lives together. Then my children as they are my greatest gift and responsibility. Then my career as it brings me gratitude for what I feel I contribute to this world. That's it for now. I do not feel guilty anymore about not volunteering my time or cutting out friends who suck up time with their drama. It's not for me to feel bad about valuing and prioritizing what is important to me. It's not selfish. I'm a grown-up and it's my decision.

So many people say they don't want to grow up due to the responsibility and anxiety it brings but it has done just the opposite for me. It has been freeing. There is nothing in my life I have not chosen and when I feel down or anxious or insecure I just remember that it's for me to control. It's for me to grow up.

Simplicity Principles

- We only desire what we want and need out of life. *Living with intention, I ask myself, Why am I doing this? Do I need this? Does this bring me joy?*
- Mental creation always precedes physical creation. Before a building is physically constructed, there's a blueprint.
- Thought becomes life.
- Do not major in the minor things.
- Focusing on competing and beating others to the punch is a "lack" mentality – an assumption that there isn't enough to go around.
- If your life is not carefully curated for you and by you, then you are living someone else's life.
- Walking through life numb from pacifiers, addictions and distractions is easy. But the avoidance of pain is a mistake. All mistakes lead to our greatest revelations and greatest joys. There is no love without loss.
- The unexamined life is not worth living. But it's important to note that if all you do is examine your life to tedium then you are not living either.

- Living a life of service is a fulfilling life, but first we must serve ourselves. Then, we must focus outward and ask, How can I serve others? If you make other people happy, you will feel happier.
- There is no right or wrong path.
- There is so much to be happy for when we take moments to stop and notice.
- You are a creator. We all are. Filling our days with distractions hides our potential. A fear-based society holds us back from showing what our minds can do. But, we need you to be you. Shut off the electronics. Stop the twitch. Embrace simplicity. Let your mind wander and come up with brilliant ideas. The world needs innovators and thinkers. Our children need you to set an example for them.
- Your thoughts are the blueprint of the life you are building one day at a time
- You are the designer of your destiny
- Our true excellence comes from our own story, our own self-expression and following our own path
- When we are true to the core of ourselves and honor our values and do activities that are congruent with our essence, then we become unstoppable.

Simplicity Principles

- Seeking someone else's approval and basing our life around someone else's opinion is one of the most debilitating of human afflictions.
- Your happiness shouldn't derive from the fear-based opinions of those riddled with self-limiting beliefs on joy, love and abundance
- The more we are US, the more we elevate our very existence.
- Look at every action you take and ask yourself, "Why am I doing this?"

Acknowledgments

Ken, Sophia and Cash- You three are my EVERYTHING. I love you so much. Ken, thank you for being my rock, my voice of reason and my biggest fan. I couldn't do any of this without you by my side. I'm so grateful to have you as my partner through life. Sophia and Cash, thank you for letting me be your mommy. You have completed me and made me the happiest person in the world. I love spending my life with you! I love you guys!

Mom, Dad and Lorene- Thank you for loving me unconditionally and raising me with kindness. The greatest gift you've given me is the gift of love that I'm passing on to my children and whomever I meet. Love is the most important gift to share with the world. I love you!

Kristi- My best friend, now sister. From the MICU to introducing me to your brother. Thank you for your years of love and friendship. Here is your official pat on the back in print. Love you!

Melissa, Irene, Ken, Calvin- Family. I'm grateful for your love and support. I love you!

Laura, Leahann, and Stacy- Sisters by choice. Thank you for the talks, the fun, the memories and being such grounding forces to keep me balanced.

Lori- My success partner and friend. Thank you for being my sounding board, pushing me and believing in me.

Rodney- Your mentorship and insight has been everything. I cannot tell you how much your guidance and belief in me has helped. Thank you for your honesty and help.

Frank- With your feedback and input this book came together. I couldn't believe you accepted my manuscript and am honored you joined me on this project. Your kind words and intelligent insight gave me the courage to complete this book. Thank you!

Delina and the APM- Thank you for your wisdom and support. Writing The Choice with you has been life changing and I'm excited for many more adventures and growth with you.

Julie, Olivia, Brenna, Kristina, Danielle, Megan, Lisa, Jeanie- Thank you for an amazing Joy Of Living Retreat.

Acknowledgments

What a beautiful week in Costa Rica. You'll never know how much that helped me finish this book! I look forward to many more retreats and a lifetime of friendship.

All the families that took me in and made me a part of yours- thank you.

The women that contributed letters- Thank you for sharing a part of your heart with us.

Friends from across the globe- thank you for being a part of my life, my story and my heart.

To you, dear reader- Wow, thank you for reading this piece of me. I hope that it brings you joy.

About Gretchen

Gretchen Stewart uplifts the world with her writing and speaking sharing unique insights that have brought her joy, purpose and peace. She is the founder of Sunshine Press and the author of multiple bestselling books. Hosting Joy Of Living Masterminds and Retreats in exotic locations worldwide, she is able to help transform others with her indomitable spirit. From the innovative philosophy of her "Joy Manifesto," to her published books on overcoming challenges and finding joy, to inspirational speaking; Gretchen is an unstoppable dervish of positivity. She lives in sunny Florida with her amazing husband and two beautiful children.